The Overthinker's Guide To Relationship Communication

How To Stop Analyzing Every Word • Break The Cycle Of Doubt And Deepen Bonds • Tools To Build Trust, Openness, And Clarity

Sage Lifestyle Press

Sage Lifestyle Press

© **Copyright Sage Lifestyle Press, 2024 - All rights reserved.**

The content within this book may not be reproduced, duplicated or transmitted without direct written permission from the author or the publisher.

Under no circumstances will any blame or legal responsibility be held against the publisher, or author, for any damages, reparation, or monetary loss due to the information contained within this book. Either directly or indirectly. You are responsible for your own choices, actions, and results.

Legal Notice:

This book is copyright protected. This book is only for personal use. You cannot amend, distribute, sell, use, quote or paraphrase any part, of the content within this book, without the consent of the author or publisher.

Disclaimer Notice:

Please note the information contained within this document is for educational and entertainment purposes only. All effort has been expended to present accurate, up-to-date, and reliable, complete information. No warranties of any kind are declared or implied. Readers acknowledge that the author is not engaging in the rendering of legal, financial, medical or professional advice. The content within this book has been derived from various sources. Please consult a licensed professional before attempting any techniques outlined in this book.

By reading this document, the reader agrees that under no circumstances is the author responsible for any losses, direct or indirect, which are incurred as a result of the use of the information contained within this document, including, but not limited to, — errors, omissions, or inaccuracies.

Contents

Introduction	V
1. Understanding the Roots of Overthinking	1
2. Emotional Intelligence and Self-Awareness	17
3. Mindfulness for Overthinkers	33
4. Building Effective Communication Skills	45
5. Overcoming Relationship Anxiety	61
Unlock the Power of Generosity	77
6. Personal Growth and Self-Reflection	81
7. Strategies for Long-Term Relationship Health	99
8. Cultural Sensitivity and Embracing Differences	115
9. Healing and Wholeness—The Way Back to Yourself	133
Keeping the Connection Strong	143
Quick Start Guide	145
QUIZ: Is Overthinking Hurting Your Relationship?	149
Conclusion	153
References	155

Introduction

Do you ever replay certain moments or conversations over and over—why didn't he say why he left? Was it because of her? Is he searching for someone more beautiful? More exciting? More effortless? Each question lingers, unanswered.

Consider Kylee, who has these thoughts swirling like autumn leaves caught in an eddy, each one a different shade of doubt. She sits at her kitchen table, a cold cup of coffee forgotten before her, as the late afternoon sun paints long shadows across the linoleum floor. The clock on the wall ticks steadily, a metronome keeping time with her racing heart.

Kylee picks up her phone, her thumb hovering over his name in her contacts. Delete? Block? Call? The options dance before her eyes, each a door to a different future. Face-down, she sets the phone down as if trying to hide from its judgmental gaze.

This is the moment she realizes she has been here before, not in this exact kitchen, with its peeling wallpaper and the faint smell of last night's takeout, but in this mental space. This labyrinth of uncertainties and regrets is constructed brick by brick and neuron by firing neuron.

She stands up, the chair scraping against the floor with a sound that echoes in the empty apartment. She walks to the window and presses her forehead against the cool glass. Outside, life goes on. A couple walks hand in hand, lost in conversation. A child chases a butterfly, laughter bubbling up like a clear spring.

And here she is, trapped in the prison of her own making, analyzing every word, every glance, every silence. The clear mind she seeks appears as distant as the horizon, obscured by the fog of overthinking. Overthinking is defined by the Merrium-Webster dictionary as: "to think too much about (something): to put too much time into thinking about or analyzing (something) in a way that is more harmful than helpful. overthink a situation/problem. Someone who overthinks and worries too much."

Could there be a way out? What if she learned to quiet her thoughts and see the world more clearly? What if the key to a healthy relationship isn't dissecting the past but embracing the present?

We begin with questions, not answers, and embrace curiosity, for understanding starts with a moment of awareness. Choose to stop passively observing your life. Stop letting your overactive mind write stories that may never come true, and start learning how to live, love, and connect with a clear mind.

Learn how to take the first step together.

Chapter One

Understanding the Roots of Overthinking

"A crowded mind, Leaves no space, for a peaceful heart." - Christine Evangelou

A nervous system at ease allows you to tap into your natural tendency to be gentle at heart, in spirit, and in your approach to the world. It's a state of being that feels as rare and precious as morning dew on a summer leaf.

Close your eyes and remember the last time you felt that way. Was it last week? Last year? Or maybe before you knew the taste of heartbreak or the weight of expectations? The memory is like a faded photograph: You're sitting on a beach, your toes buried in warm sand, watching the sun melt into the horizon. The sky is a canvas of oranges and purples, and for a moment, just a moment, your mind is as calm as the sea.

But that was then, and this is now. Now, your thoughts are like a flock of startled birds taking flight at the slightest disturbance. Each "what if" and "if only" sends them scattering in a hundred different directions. The clarity you long for seems like a distant shore, obscured by the fog of your mind.

You might look down at your hands, noticing how tightly you've been gripping the edge of your chair, consciously relaxing your fingers, one by one, and taking a deep breath. The simple act can appear as a minor defiance against the chaos of the mind.

What would it be like to move through life with that ease again and approach love, work, and dreams with ease instead of clenched fists? To trust in the flow of life instead of trying to control every eddy and current? Realize that perhaps the first step towards understanding is not to grasp answers but to create space for the questions themselves.

So you take another breath, deeper this time, and look inward: look deep within as an attempt to unravel the tangled threads of thought that have woven themselves into the fabric of your days and nights.

Understanding the Roots of Overthinking

Love is exciting, especially when it is still new. The texting back and forth, the butterflies in your stomach when you see their name pop up on your phone, and how time seems to stand still when you're together is intoxicating, but then, almost imperceptibly, something shifts. You find yourself staring at your phone, wondering why they haven't texted back in the last hour. You replay your last conversation in your head, analyzing every word, every inflection. Did you say something wrong? Are they losing interest? And just like that, the excitement gets tinged with anxiety, and a knot of fear forms in your gut.

Many of us find ourselves in this state of overthinking, often without realizing how we got there. You're not alone, but to understand why and how this self-sabotaging overthinking can show up, we'll need to learn to recognize some of its subtle signs.

Let's start here!

You're out with your partner, having a great time; they're laughing at your jokes, holding your hand, being attentive, but you're still there asking them, *"Do you really love me?"* or *"Are you sure I look okay in this outfit?"* Sound familiar? Mary has been dating Tom for about six months. Things have been going well, but she can't stop thinking about the need to know Tom's emotions.

"Do you still love me?" she asks, sometimes multiple times daily. Tom, patient as he is, always responds with a smile and says, "Of course I do." However, no matter how often Tom reassures her, Mary's doubts always creep back in.

Now, it's normal to seek validation from our partners occasionally. We're humans, but when it becomes a constant need, like in Mary's case, it's a sign that overthinking has taken root. This behavior often stems from deep-seated insecurities or past experiences where we felt undervalued. The tricky part? While seeking reassurance might provide temporary relief, it feeds into a cycle of doubt. Each time Mary asks for reassurance, she's strengthening her belief that she requires external validation to be at ease in her relationship.

Another classic sign of overthinking is mind-reading assumptions. We've all been there. Your partner is quieter than usual during dinner, and suddenly, your mind is racing: Are they mad at you? Did you forget an important date? Are they thinking about breaking up?

Take Jim, for example. He sees his girlfriend, Sarah, texting late at night. Instead of asking her about it, he immediately assumes she must be hiding something. She might be talking to a former partner or misleading him. He spends a few days analyzing his partner's every move, looking for signs to confirm his suspicions. The reality? Sarah was helping her sister plan a surprise party for their mom.

This mind-reading game is dangerous because it replaces honest communication with imagined scenarios. Instead of having an open conversation with Sarah, Jim lets his assumptions fester, creating distance and mistrust where there is none. The irony is that while Jim thought he was getting closer to the truth; he pushed Sarah away.

Dwelling on details excessively is another sign of overthinking in relationships. It's like putting every interaction under a microscope, magnifying insignificant details until they become distorted and unrecognizable.

Consider Nick, whose partner forgot their six-month anniversary. In a healthy mindset, he might feel a moment of disappointment while understanding that people make mistakes. Instead, he falls into a spiral of overthinking, meticulously analyzing every interaction they've had over the past month.

He questions everything: Has his partner been less affectionate lately? Are they spending less time together? What started as a simple oversight transforms into perceived evidence of a relationship in crisis? This tendency to over-analyze can turn minor bumps into seemingly insurmountable obstacles. It's like navigating a relationship while wearing magnifying glasses—every minor detail becomes distorted and more threatening than it truly is. The real challenge lies in learning to step back and view the situation through a wider lens, allowing for a more balanced perspective.

The persistent nature of these patterns often stems from deeply ingrained experiences and beliefs. Our past relationships, family dynamics, and societal influences shape our perception of love and partnership. Think about how past betrayals might lead to hypervigilance in future relationships or how witnessing unstable relationships during formative years could instill a belief that love is inherently fragile. These underlying narratives don't just disappear; they color our interpretations and reactions, fueling the cycle of overthinking.

And no, the goal is not to eliminate all relationship-related thoughts or concerns, but to build a strong mindset to resist the lies embedded in excessive rumination. This balance is critical to maintaining both emotional well-being and relationship health.

The Impact of Past Relationship Experiences on Current Ones

You can't change your past, but you can understand how it shapes your present. Your past relationships, both romantic and familial, create a lens through which you view your current partnerships. Often clouded by unresolved issues and emotional scars, this lens can significantly impact your ability to form and maintain healthy connections.

Betrayal

The sting of betrayal would be much less painful if it killed the love that came before it, but it doesn't. Instead, it leaves you in a confusing limbo, where love and hurt coexist and trust and suspicion wage a constant battle in your mind.

Betrayal in relationships isn't limited to infidelity. It can manifest as broken promises, emotional affairs, financial deceit, or a fundamental breach of agreed-upon boundaries. Each form carries its unique pain, but they all share a common thread—they shatter the foundation of trust upon which relationships are built.

When you experience betrayal, your brain's alarm system, the amygdala, goes into overdrive. It sees threats everywhere, even in the most innocent situations. That text your partner is smiling at? It must be from someone else. Are they working late again? Surely, they're lying. This hypervigilance, while initially a protective mechanism, often backfires, creating a cycle of anxiety and mistrust.

The amygdala's activation not only fuels hypervigilance but also triggers the cognitive component of anxiety, amplifying the mind's tendency to catastrophize and expect the worst. Your brain becomes a detective, piecing together evidence of betrayal even when none exists. This constant state of alertness affects your ability to relax, contributing to a sense of persistent unease. The close relationship between hypervigilance and physical health can have a significant impact on the dynamics of a committed partnership. Being "on guard" for any potential or perceived danger that might threaten health can lead to an increase in otherwise safe-stress moments.

While acute vigilance seems protective, it drains the body's (and relationship's) resources. Auto-piloting the unrelenting "fight or flight" mode tires the circuits—both physical and mental. The primary threats to health that might emerge from "health-seeking" in a hypervigilant state seem to be emotional burnout and relationship meltdown.

The psychological impact fundamentally alters your worldview and sense of self as well, because the person you thought you knew better than anyone else suddenly becomes a stranger, leading to profound confusion and self-doubt. You find yourself questioning your judgment, wondering how you could have been wrong about someone.

This cognitive dissonance—the struggle to reconcile the person you loved with the person who hurt you—can strike at the heart of your self-esteem. Intrusive thoughts like *"Was I not good enough?"* or *"What does the other person have that I don't?"* These thoughts chip away at your sense of value, making you perceive yourself as lacking or undeserving of affection.

It's also a grief-filled process because it requires you to mourn both the loss of the relationship and your belief in the relationship; the future you had envisioned suddenly evaporates, leaving you to grapple with a new, uncertain reality. Sitting and accepting various responses makes you realize your reactions are normal in an abnormal situation. It's your psyche's way of processing a profound hurt and trying to protect you from future pain.

While these responses are normal, they don't have to be permanent. With time, self-reflection, and often professional help, it's possible to process the betrayal and move forward.

Attachment Style

How you form bonds with others is the blueprint for connecting with others, especially in intimate relationships. It's not about how you express love, but how you form emotional bonds and respond to closeness or distance. This pattern is shaped in your early years through interactions with your primary caregivers, creating a template that often persists into adulthood, influencing your romantic relationships in significant ways.

Secure attachment: This is the healthiest of the four styles. You're comfortable with intimacy and independence if you have a secure attachment. You trust easily, communicate emotions effectively, and form stable, satisfying connections. In relationships, you can offer support and seek it when needed, resolving conflicts constructively.

Anxious attachment: If you have an anxious attachment style, you crave intimacy and closeness but fear abandonment and rejection.

These traits may be familiar to you:

- Seek constant reassurance from your partner.
- Become overly sensitive to your partner's moods and behaviors.
- Be prone to jealousy and relationship anxiety.

Avoidant attachment: Those with an avoidant attachment style value independence above all else and may be uncomfortable with deep emotional intimacy. In relationships, you might recognize these traits:

- Seeming distant or emotionally unavailable.

- Struggling to commit or express feelings.

- Withdrawing when relationships start to deepen.

Disorganized attachment: Also known as fearful-avoidant, this style often stems from a history of trauma or neglect. If you have this attachment style, you desire close relationships but fear getting hurt.

Disorganized attachment can lead to:

- Unpredictable or erratic behavior in relationships.

- Difficulty trusting others and regulating emotions.

- Alternating between anxious and avoidant behaviors.

Understanding your attachment style is excellent for self-awareness and growth in relationships. If you recognize anxious patterns in yourself, you might notice a tendency to seek constant reassurance, interpreting normal fluctuations in attention as signs of abandonment. Those with avoidant tendencies may struggle with emotional intimacy, withdrawing when a relationship starts to deepen.

These styles are not fixed destinies. With a bit of self-reflection, effort, and sometimes professional help, you can gravitate toward a more secure attachment style; it's a matter of challenging ingrained beliefs about relationships, learning new ways of communicating, and gradually becoming more comfortable with intimacy and independence.

Idealized Relationships

Do you feel as though everywhere you look, you only see happy couples who seem to be going on some holiday or adventure together? These couples finish each other's sentences with a laugh, couples whose Instagram feeds are a constant stream of candlelit dinners and surprise gifts. It's enough to make you wonder: Is everyone else living in a romantic comedy while you're stuck in a reality show?

The truth is that these picture-perfect relationships we see, whether in media, social networks, or even among our friends, are often carefully curated versions of reality. They're highlight reels, not behind-the-scenes footage. These idealized portrayals often create a benchmark that's not just unrealistic—it's often downright impossible. They propose the absence of disagreements, constant elation, and an unending state of joy characterizing true love. In truth, those versions are one sided, and regardless of what is posted online, it's how we interpret these signs or signals that affect our thoughts and moods.

When you're constantly comparing your relationship to these polished versions, you're setting yourself up for disappointment; that argument you had with your partner about whose turn it is to do the dishes? Now, it seems like a signal that your relationship is failing instead of being a typical part of living together. The peaceful night dedicated to Netflix? It may appear insufficient, contrasted with the grand gestures exhibited online.

This comparison game feeds directly into overthinking and anxiety. You might find yourself constantly analyzing your relationship, looking for signs that it measures up to the ideal. Am I loved enough if my partner doesn't surprise me with flowers every week? Are we happy enough if we're not always posting a couple of selfies? This overthinking can create problems where none existed, straining the relationship with unnecessary pressure.

Real relationships are complex, multifaceted, and, yes, imperfect. They involve two human beings with flaws, quirks, and bad days. The strength of these relationships lies in the support we give and receive, understanding, and growing together through the highs and lows. In the small moments, there are the inside jokes, the comfort of silence, and the support during tough times. It's in the willingness to work through disagreements, the ability to apologize and forgive, and the choice to keep choosing each other daily.

Your experiences don't have to define your future relationships, but understanding their impact is the first step toward creating healthier patterns. It's not about erasing your past but about recognizing how it influences your present and using that awareness to foster more fulfilling, anxiety-free connections.

Pause to contemplate:

- Can you identify a recurring theme in your past relationships that seems to repeat in your current one?

- How do you think your childhood experiences shaped your romantic relationship expectations?

This is important, because childhood memories play a powerful role in shaping our adult perspectives, often blending actual events with the meanings we attached to them as children. This fusion can color our decision-making and worldviews, as we interpret present experiences through the lens of our younger selves. When childhood perceptions and interpretations remain unexamined, they can subtly influence our adult responses, shaping how we react, connect, and view the world around us. Recognizing this dynamic can open pathways to greater self-awareness, allowing us to separate past meanings from present realities.

- If you experience anxiety in your relationship, can you link that feeling to a past experience?

- In what ways do you think societal or media portrayals of 'perfect' relationships have influenced your view of love?

- Can you recall a moment when you reacted to your current partner based on a past hurt rather than the present situation?

Recognize the Role of Fear and Insecurity in Over-analyzing Partner Behavior

Most of us have googled something like: "What does it mean if the person I'm dating hasn't texted back in three hours?" or "Why didn't they say 'I love you' back right away?" These moments of doubt and anxiety are more common than we might think, rooted in the fears and insecurities that we all carry into our relationships.

Fear of Abandonment

Nina's therapist told her during one of her sessions, "Your fear of abandonment comes from a place of deep-seated vulnerability." She wanted to roll her eyes, but then she heard the therapist say, "It's not about weakness. It's about the depth of your care and how deeply you feel about connections."

Does that hit home? It made Nina realize that this fear, this constant worry that the people she loves might leave, isn't just some irrational thought. It's an authentic, very human experience. It's the part of us that remembers every goodbye, every lost connection, every time we felt left behind. This hypervigilance, this constant state of alert, robs us of the joy of the present moment and of enjoying the space and time to be with the person we love.

So, how do we move past this? We learn to ground ourselves in the now—the warmth of our partner's smile, the comfort of their touch, the sound of their laughter. It's about building a library of positive experiences to counterbalance the archive of past hurts, and perhaps most importantly, we muster the strength to be vulnerable. To say, "Hey, I'm dealing with insecurities right now," or "I'm worried about us." It's scary to put our fears out there. But in my experience, we often find the reassurance we're looking for in these moments of open, honest communication.

Acknowledge painful emotions without letting them control you; the risk of loss in deep love is worth the beauty of connection.

Fear and insecurity often play a significant role in over-analyzing a partner's behavior. When past experiences have disrupted trust or stability—whether from betrayal, childhood trauma, or previous unhealthy relationships—these "broken patterns" can create insecurities that linger beneath the surface. Your mind may become hyper-aware of potential threats, constantly scanning for signs of trouble, even when none exists.

For example, imagine a scenario where your partner is unusually quiet after work. Instead of assuming they had a tough day, your insecurities might convince you they are upset with you or hiding something. This response is not just about the present situation; it reflects past experiences where silence may have preceded conflict or deception. By recognizing this pattern, you can separate past fears from present realities, offering yourself a chance to respond with curiosity and compassion instead of anxiety and suspicion. This awareness not only reduces over-analysis but also fosters healthier, more open communication with your partner.

Low Self-Esteem

People often say, "Know your worth," but what does that mean when you've always felt insufficient? When my partner compliments me, this little voice in my head says, "They're just being nice when they choose to spend time with me." I can't help but wonder, "Are they here willingly, or are they under pressure?" It's exhausting because no matter how much love and affirmation pour in, it never seems enough.

The tricky part is that this isn't just about how we see ourselves. It spills over into how we interpret every interaction in our relationships. A delayed response to a text becomes proof that we're not a priority. A casual comment gets dissected for hidden meanings, usually negative ones. We become detectives, always looking for evidence confirming our worst fears about ourselves.

We build our self-esteem by gradually changing the narrative we tell ourselves. Start challenging that critical inner voice that is always ready to tear us down. Start with small steps. Keep a journal of things you did well during the day, no matter how minor. Practice accepting compliments with a simple "thank you" instead of immediately deflecting them. It might seem uncomfortable initially, but gradually, it will seem more natural.

Start taking your partner's words and actions at face value in your relationships. It's not easy, and some days are more complicated than others. This understanding can help you stop repeatedly questioning their affection, allowing you to draw closer to the love you truly desire rather than distancing yourself from it.

Intimacy Insecurities

Intimacy is a lot of things. It is, for one, that physical connection that you have with your partner, the comfort of a familiar touch, and the warmth of a hug. It's also the emotional nakedness of sharing your deepest fears, the trust fall of revealing your true self, scars, and all.

Think about moments when you may be physically near but emotionally distant when insecurities prevent you from expressing your genuine thoughts. If you allow these fears to control you, an invisible wall will form between you and your partner; over time, it becomes a barrier.

That's the paradox of intimacy and insecurities. We crave closeness, yet we fear it. We want to be fully known and accepted, yet we're terrified of rejection. So we do this dance—one step forward, two steps back. We might hesitate to start intimacy, physical or emotional. We might withdraw when conversations get too deep and emotions become too intense. From the outside, it might look like disinterest or coldness. But inside, it's a storm of conflicting desires and fears. We want to dive deep, but we're afraid of drowning.

Attachment styles play a significant role in how we navigate this paradox. Those with an anxious attachment style may find themselves over-seeking reassurance, feeling that any distance is a sign of impending rejection.

Individuals with an avoidant attachment style might struggle to open up, equating vulnerability with a loss of independence or control. Even those with a secure attachment style are not immune to moments of insecurity, especially when past experiences have sown seeds of doubt.

For example, someone with an anxious attachment style might interpret a partner's quietness as a sign of disinterest, leading to a cycle of seeking validation and feeling unfulfilled. Meanwhile, an avoidant partner might react to emotional closeness by pulling away, not because they don't care, but because intimacy triggers a deeply rooted fear of vulnerability. Understanding how attachment styles influence these reactions can help both partners recognize when insecurities, not reality, are driving their behaviors.

So, how do we deal with this? It starts with self-acknowledgment, looking in the mirror and saying, "Yes, I'm afraid of being hurt. Yes, I have trouble accepting that I'm worthy of love. And that's okay." The next step, and often the hardest, is sharing these feelings with our partner. And you know what? Instead of rejection, you may be surprised to be met with understanding and empathy.

Sometimes insecurity whispers doubts, and the urge to withdraw feels overwhelming. But now, instead of giving in to those impulses, try leaning into the discomfort. Remind yourself that your quirks, fears, and unique traits are all part of who you are—worthy of love, not despite their uniqueness, but because of it. When you understand your attachment style, you can break the cycle of push and pull, allowing intimacy to flow naturally and authentically.[1]

---

1. The Complete Guide To Attachment Styles: Learn to Navigate Anxious and Avoidant Patterns - How to Build Trust and Connection - Break Through Barriers to Vulnerability - Tools and Techniques-by Sage Lifestyle Press

Chapter Two

Emotional Intelligence and Self-Awareness

Emotional intelligence (EI) and self-awareness are the bedrock of every healthy relationship, including the one you have with yourself. However, no "Dummies Guide" can magically make you into a beacon of self-awareness overnight. EI in relationships is the ability to understand, interpret, and manage your own emotions. It fosters empathy, clear communication, and mutual respect, helping your person respond thoughtfully rather than react impulsively, ultimately strengthening the connection and trust within the relationship.

Additionally, EI and optimism are closely intertwined, forming a dynamic duo that shapes our outlook on life and our ability to handle its challenges. But don't expect to turn into an eternal optimist overnight. EI—the capacity to understand, regulate, and harness emotions—feeds optimism by allowing you to reframe setbacks and view adversity as an opportunity. It's what helps you respond to life's curveballs with a sense of resilience and hope rather than succumbing to despair. So the good news is by doing this work, you may also find you are more optimistic.

Developing this skill isn't a polished, Instagram-ready journey. It's a raw, unfiltered dive into how your thoughts and emotions work together—or against each other. It's sitting with disappointment when optimism feels elusive and choosing, anyway, to see a silver lining. Think of how often we're told to "just be positive" as if optimism is a switch you can flip. The truth is, optimism grows from doing the hard work of understanding your emotional responses and reinterpreting them in constructive ways. While often uncomfortable, it requires you to peel back the layers of your psyche, facing the good, the bad, and the downright ugly. It's learning to sit with your emotions, even when they're pushing you to run and hide. It's about understanding why you do what you do, even when what you do makes no sense.

You might notice it in the small moments—when your reaction to a simple text feels bigger than it should be. When a casual comment from your partner brushes against an old wound you thought had healed. When you fall into patterns, you swore you'd outgrow.

Each time you look inward, you'll find another layer of yourself waiting to be understood. Some days, you'll encounter things that make you want to look away—the defenses you put up to protect yourself, the stories you told yourself about love, and how you learned to downplay yourself to align with others' expectations. On other days, you'll rediscover forgotten aspects of yourself like treasures—your capacity for joy, resilience, and ability to love deeply despite past hurts.

The hardest truth? You have to do this inner work while still living your life. While still showing up for dinner with your partner, responding to family texts, and navigating friendships and relationships that don't pause for your moments of self-discovery. Some days, it may seem easier to avoid work and continue with your familiar patterns and well-worn reactions.

Yet, each time you choose to understand yourself better, you create an opportunity for a deeper connection. Each moment of self-awareness gives you a choice—to react from old patterns or to respond from a place of understanding. This isn't about becoming a perfect partner or never making mistakes. It's about becoming more authentically yourself in your relationships.

Differentiating Thoughts and Feelings

Thoughts and feelings, aren't they the same thing, though? It's a common misconception, but understanding their differences is crucial for EI and healthier relationships. It's also a learnable skill. To differentiate thoughts from feelings, practice identifying whether your inner dialogue expresses an emotion ("I feel sad") or a belief ("I think they are ignoring me"). Regularly pause to separate facts from interpretations, build your emotional vocabulary, and reflect on your responses to improve emotional awareness and communication.

Let's break it down:

Thoughts are the mental interpretations of our experiences. They're the stories we tell ourselves about what's happening. Feelings are the emotional responses to these thoughts and experiences. They manifest as physical sensations in our bodies.

Here's a scenario we can use: Your partner forgets to call during lunch as promised. Your immediate thought might be, *"They don't care about me."* This thought then triggers feelings of hurt, disappointment, or anger.

The key is recognizing that the thought *"They don't care about me"* isn't a fact. It's an interpretation. And this subscribed meaning leads to your emotional response. The total behavior comprises doing (action), thoughts, feelings, and physiology, which can occur simultaneously, which makes the entire process difficult to traverse. By separating thoughts from feelings, we gain more control over our reactions. Here's how you can start practicing this:

1. Identify the situation: What actually happened?

2. Recognize your thoughts: What are you saying to yourself about this situation?

3. Name your feelings: What emotions are you experiencing?

4. Notice physical sensations: How are these feelings manifesting in your body?

This process helps create space between the event, your interpretation, and your emotional response. It allows you to question your thoughts before they spiral into intense emotions.

For example, instead of immediately reacting with anger when your partner forgets to call, you might pause and think:

1. Situation: My partner didn't call during lunch.

2. Thought: "I don't matter to them." (Is this really true? Are there other possibilities?)

3. Feeling: Hurt, disappointed.

4. Physical sensation: Tightness in chest, clenched jaw.

By breaking it down this way, you're more likely to respond thoughtfully rather than react impulsively.

This skill takes practice. Start by focusing on your thoughts and feelings in less emotionally charged situations. You can apply this to more challenging relationship scenarios as you become more adept.

Instead of accusing your partner of not caring, you can express yourself more clearly: "When you didn't call, I felt hurt and disappointed because I thought you might not care." This approach opens the door to more productive conversations and deeper understanding in your relationships. It's not about perfection, but about developing greater awareness and choosing more intentional responses.

What are your thoughts on this? Can you recall a recent situation where you might have benefited from separating your thoughts from your feelings?

Influence of Self-Perception on Communication

The saying "Confidence is quiet" is a popular modern adage often attributed to the general idea that truly confident individuals do not need to boast or draw attention to themselves. While there is no definitive origin or specific author, this concept aligns with the broader philosophies of stoicism, humility, and emotional intelligence. It is frequently used in self-help, leadership, and personal development contexts to illustrate the contrast between genuine self-assurance and the need for external validation. But honestly, how many of us feel that way, especially in love and relationships? There are many day to day barriers to us having this kind of "quiet" confidence. Consider this limited list of likely culprits:

- **Societal Standards and Media Influence**: Constant exposure to idealized images and lifestyles through media can create unrealistic standards for appearance, success, and relationships. This pressure often makes us feel like they don't measure up, leading to self-doubt.

- **Cultural Expectations**: Different cultures have unique expectations around appearance, behavior, and success. These can be restrictive, especially if someone's authentic self doesn't align with these norms, making it difficult to feel accepted and comfortable.

- **Judgment and Comparison**: The tendency to compare ourselves to others, often amplified by social media, can erode self-confidence. Seeing selective and idealized versions of others' lives can make us feel inadequate or insecure.

Our self-perception significantly influences how we communicate with our partners. It affects not just what we say but how we say it and even what we choose not to say.

Consider a situation where you need to discuss something meaningful with your partner. If you have a positive self-perception, you're more likely to approach the conversation directly, expressing your thoughts and feelings clearly. You might say, "I felt hurt when you forgot our plans. Can we talk about it?" This approach stems from believing your feelings are valid and deserve to be heard.

On the other hand, if you're struggling with self-doubt, you might find yourself avoiding the conversation altogether or expressing yourself indirectly. You might say, "It's fine, don't worry about it," while clearly not being fine. This indirect communication often leads to misunderstandings and unresolved feelings.

Self-perception also manifests in our non-verbal communication. Non-verbal cues such as body language, tone of voice, and facial expressions convey messages that reinforce or contradict our words. Someone with high self-esteem typically maintains eye contact, uses open gestures, and speaks with a clear, steady voice. In contrast, low self-esteem might result in hunched shoulders, averted gaze, or a hesitant tone.

Improving how we communicate in relationships starts with developing self-awareness. Here are some practical steps:

1. Observe your internal dialogue. What are you telling yourself about your worth and right to be heard in the relationship?

2. Challenge negative self-talk. Would you speak to a friend the way you talk to yourself?

3. Practice expressing yourself clearly, starting with low-stakes conversations. Gradually work up to more significant issues.

4. Pay attention to your body language. Before meaningful conversations, consciously adjust your posture. Stand or sit up straight, uncross your arms, and take deep breaths to help you be more assured.

5. Focus on active listening. Show your partner you value their perspective by giving them your full attention when they speak.

6. Ask for feedback. Encourage your partner to share how they perceive your communication style. This can provide valuable insights and areas for improvement.

Confident communication is believing in the validity of your thoughts and emotions, being brave enough to show them as authentically as possible while acknowledging that you are flawed and possess areas where you sometimes fall short. This realization is ok - give yourself a break.

Cultivating Empathy for Partner Perspectives

Empathy allows for a compassionate response that recognizes and validates your partner's emotions, which strengthens trust and emotional connection. In a healthy relationship, empathy enables both partners to feel seen, understood, and supported, fostering a safe space where each person is valued.

In romantic relationships, this becomes even more crucial because we're not just trying to understand random experiences—we're trying to understand the person we've chosen to share our life with. Their joys become our joys, their pain touches our hearts, and their struggles matter to us.

What Real Empathy Looks Like

Known for their engaging storytelling, rich character development, and high production quality, Korean dramas have become hugely popular worldwide. They often cover a wide range of genres, including romance, thriller, fantasy, historical, and slice-of-life, making them versatile and appealing to diverse audiences. They frequently explore themes of love, friendship, family, and personal growth.

They can teach us to read the unspoken language of emotions without realizing it. This lesson becomes particularly powerful when your partner comes home carrying the weight of a difficult day. You can see it in the slight drop of their shoulders, hear it in the heavy sigh as they close the door, and sense it in the unusual quiet that fills the room.

In these moments, true presence matters more than perfect words. It's about tuning in to what isn't being said:

- The project deadline makes them question their competence.

- The office politics remind them of past workplace trauma.

- The feedback that has touched on their deepest insecurities.

- The decision they're wrestling with that keeps them up at night.

Often, our instinct is to jump in with solutions or minimize their struggles with phrases like "It'll get better" or "At least you have a job." We think we're helping, but, in truth, we're trying to make ourselves more comfortable with their discomfort. And, in reality, showing a lack of empathy. I recall once in marriage therapy, the counselor telling us that we should be each other's biggest fan. If one of us came home venting, saying something like, "My boss is a jerk," the best response would be, "She certainly is!" That is some of the best advice our relationship has ever received.

Showing genuine empathy would be for us to sit in that discomfort with them, to understand that today's frustration might be tangled up with the time they were passed over for promotion last year or the childhood message that they're never quite good enough. It means recognizing that sometimes people need a break to process their emotions before they can start working on solutions. Both partners need to be open to share in this space together, creating a safe environment where vulnerability is met with understanding. Try saying, let me share the weight of what you're feeling. I don't have solutions to offer—only my presence, my shoulder, my understanding. No matter what storm you're facing, you don't have to weather it alone.

What your partner needs might vary—sometimes, it's a quiet presence while they process, and other times, it's active engagement in problem-solving. The key is tuning in to their needs rather than imposing our idea of support.

Building Your Empathy Muscles

Notice if you are impatient and may be too quick to offer solutions when someone just needs you to listen. Sometimes, rushing to fix things was more about discomfort with difficult emotions than about helping the other person.

Learning to sit with our emotional world opens the door to understanding others. When you recognize your patterns—how criticism makes your chest tight, how stress shows up as irritability, why certain words trigger old memories—you develop a map for understanding others' emotional terrain.

This awareness transforms how you show up in relationships. You begin to see the small changes in your partner's energy. You learn to read the silence between their words, to understand that a sharp response might be due to fear and withdrawal from being overwhelmed.

Creating space for vulnerability becomes natural when you've learned to hold space for your complicated feelings. You recognize that sometimes your partner must voice their fears without hearing solutions, express anger without being fixed, and share dreams without judgment.

The real gift of empathy lies in these quiet moments of understanding. It's in the gentle nod that says, "I hear you." It's in how you adjust your approach based on your partner's needs—whether that's a listening ear, a warm embrace, or simply sitting together in comfortable silence.

Empathy Without Boundaries

Empathy without boundaries is cruelty. It isn't kind when you absorb your partner's every emotion until you can no longer distinguish between your feelings. It's cruel to them when your over involvement in their emotional world prevents them from developing their emotional strength.

Genuine empathy requires enough distance to see clearly. Imagine being with someone you deeply care for in distress—you can offer your support, understand their suffering, and stay strong enough to be genuinely helpful. You don't jump into the river of their emotions; you remain on the bank where you can throw them a lifeline.

This balance allows you to care deeply while maintaining your emotional well-being. You can understand your partner's work frustration without taking responsibility for solving it. You can acknowledge their family struggles without becoming entangled in dynamics that aren't yours to fix.

Healthy empathy means recognizing where you end and your partner begins. It means understanding that sometimes the most empathetic response is stepping back to allow them space to process their emotions. It means knowing when to listen, when to support, and when to encourage them to seek additional help. Your role in your partner's emotional life isn't to be their savior but their witness—present, understanding, and supportive while remaining anchored in your emotional ground.

Learning Where to Draw the Lines

There's a difference between standing with someone in their pain and carrying their pain for them. Do you sometimes lie awake at night, worrying about your friend's marriage problems, strategizing solutions for your partner's work challenges, and absorbing everyone's emotional struggles until they identify with your feelings?

True empathy requires boundaries. We don't just witness others' pain without them—we begin to live it. We become so enmeshed in their emotional world that we lose our ability to offer real support. It's like trying to help someone out of a hole while jumping into it with them.

Supporting others while preserving our emotional well-being requires clear, compassionate language. We need words that honor both our capacity to care and our need for healthy separation. Setting boundaries around empathy looks something like this:

- "I hear how difficult this situation is, and I want to support you. Right now, I'm feeling overwhelmed. Could we pause and return to this conversation in an hour when I can be more present?"

- "I care deeply about what you're going through. This reminds me of my experiences, making it hard to see clearly. Would you be open to exploring this with a counselor who can offer better guidance?"

- "I want to understand and support you through this family conflict. At the same time, I need to step back from getting directly involved in the situation."

Creating these boundaries requires clear, gentle language:

- Instead of absorbing every emotion: "I'm here to listen and support you. What kind of support would be most helpful right now?"

- When feeling emotionally flooded: "This conversation matters to me. I need a moment to process my feelings to be fully present for yours."

- When the issue hits home: "I find that this situation stirs up strong feelings for me. I might not be the best person to help you process this challenge."

These boundaries protect both partners. They allow you to remain supportive while maintaining your emotional stability. They give your partner the gift of finding their strength rather than becoming dependent on your emotional support.

Remember: Good boundaries make deep empathy possible. They create a secure space where both partners can experience, heal, and grow—together but separately.

Practice Opportunities

Your first language shapes how you express emotion. In Mandarin, you don't say, "I am angry"; instead, you say, "My anger is coming up." In Japanese, there are dozens of words for different types of silences, each carrying its particular emotional weight. In Spanish, "te quiero" and "te amo" express different depths of love that English can't quite capture.

Understanding this helps us recognize how our cultural and linguistic backgrounds influence how we experience and express emotions. Maybe you grew up in a family where feelings were expressed through actions rather than words. Or perhaps your culture views certain emotions as private, meant to be processed alone rather than shared.

Learning your partner's emotional language might mean understanding that their long silences are a form of processing, not withdrawal. It might mean recognizing that their constant questions about your day aren't prying but their culture's way of showing care. It could mean appreciating why they must consult family about big decisions or prefer to handle certain feelings privately.

Awareness transforms how we practice empathy. Instead of assuming your partner, or anyone else, processes emotions as we do, we learn to recognize and respect different emotional dialects. We understand that empathy sometimes means giving space instead of words or offering presence instead of solutions.

I am here to hold space for every part of who you are. Nothing is as empowering as hearing those words from a partner. To be truly seen, accepted, and supported in all our complexity is a profound experience.

To hold that space for your partner, you must first do it for yourself. It's not about achieving perfection or following a prescribed path. It's about facing yourself honestly—your strengths, flaws, and contradictions. This exercise won't be comfortable. It might mean confronting aspects of yourself you've long ignored or patterns you'd rather not acknowledge. But this self-awareness becomes the bedrock of genuine connection. It allows you to show up authentically, not just for yourself but for your partner.

Remember, it's not about getting it right all the time. It's about being present, authentic, and willing to grow—alongside your partner, day by day.

EI lives in the space between your first reaction and your response. It exists in the breath you take when your partner's words bring up old hurt. It's when you become aware of your hand reaching for your phone rather than meeting their downward gaze in a challenging conversation. It's in recognizing your patterns without condemning yourself for having them.

The genuine value of self-awareness may not reside in attaining complete understanding. Perhaps it's in learning to ride the waves of your emotions without drowning in them. Accepting that some days you'll navigate your relationships gracefully, and other days you'll bump against every wall trying to find your way. Both are valid. Both are necessary. Both are teaching you something about who you are and how you love.

To recap, in order to boost your EI try these practices:

1. **Practice Active Listening**-Focus entirely on what others are saying without interrupting or planning your response. This helps you understand their emotions and perspectives better, which enhances empathy and connection.

2. **Reflect on Your Emotions Daily**-Spend a few minutes each day reflecting on your emotions and identifying what triggered them. Journaling can be particularly helpful, as it promotes awareness and helps you recognize emotional patterns over time.

3. **Develop Self-Regulation Techniques**-Practice techniques like deep breathing, mindfulness, or a quick pause when feeling intense emotions. This helps you manage reactions and respond thoughtfully instead of impulsively.

4. **Seek Constructive Feedback**-Ask trusted friends, family, or colleagues for feedback on how you handle emotions and interactions. This outside perspective can reveal blind spots and areas where you can grow.

5. **Practice Empathy in Everyday Situations**-Try to put yourself in others' shoes in daily interactions, even brief ones. Whether it's with coworkers, friends, or even a stranger, practicing empathy fosters compassion and enhances your understanding of others' emotions.

Building EI takes time and intentional practice, but these actions can lead to greater self-awareness, improved relationships, and better decision-making.

Chapter Three

Mindfulness for Overthinkers

When was the last time you were fully present with a task or enjoyed a meal and registered how it tasted, smelled, and felt in your mouth?

Imagine having lunch alone, a bowl of tomato soup, and a grilled cheese sandwich. Nothing fancy. As you take the first bite, try to imagine a shift as well. You might observe the way the sunlight streams through the window. You can actually taste your food and enjoy your surroundings.

The thing about overthinking is that it makes us so wrapped up in the narratives in our heads that we miss out on the life happening right before us. We're so busy trying to control the future or make sense of the past that we forget to live in the present. However, just focusing on your lunch won't solve all your problems. Still, when you allow yourself that brief experience of mindfulness, it is like a pebble dropped in a pond, sending out ripples of positivity that can be felt throughout the day.

What if you could bring that presence to other areas of your life? To relationships? To work? To those moments when overthinking tends to take over?

That's what this chapter is about. It is not about achieving some Zen-like state of constant calm (let's be honest, that's not happening) but about finding those small moments of presence amid our busy, thought-filled lives. It's about learning to be here, even when 'here' is uncomfortable and 'now' is challenging.

Practice Mindfulness Meditation to Calm Thought Patterns

Mindfulness is something that we hear about constantly these days. However, its prevalence in popular media doesn't diminish its significance, particularly for those prone to overthinking in relationships.

Mindfulness meditation is a practice of present-moment awareness. It involves deliberately focusing on experiences in the now, thoughts, and sensations without judgment. An overthinker dwells on past events, all while anxiously anticipating future scenarios.

To counteract this, try:

- Paying attention to a specific anchor (often the breath).
- Becoming aware of mental distractions.
- Gently returning attention to the anchor.

This seemingly simple process develops a skill vital for managing overthinking: the ability to acknowledge thoughts without becoming entangled in them.

Try this: Set a timer for 30 seconds (you can slowly increase to about 2 minutes as you get the hang of the process). Close your eyes and focus on your breath. Become aware of the air moving in and out of your nostrils or the rise and fall of your chest. When you recognize your mind straying—and it will—gently bring your attention back to your breath. Just notice that you are not focusing and then return to the practice. Don't judge yourself for getting distracted; return to focusing on your breath.

How was that? If you found your mind constantly drifting, congratulations, you've just experienced firsthand the challenge that mindfulness addresses. If you can stay focused for even a few seconds, you've taken the first step in training your mind to be more present.

Neurological Impacts and Relationship Dynamics

Have you ever noticed your partner looking at you when they thought you weren't looking? It's a mix of surprise, warmth, and a hint of bashfulness. That look tells me more than words ever could—it says, "You see me, really see me."

This level of awareness and truly noticing the small things doesn't come naturally to many of us. Maybe you are so used to being so caught up in your thoughts and anxieties about your relationship that you miss these little moments. But as you practice mindfulness, you will find yourself becoming more attuned not just to your inner world but to the subtle nuances of your partner's behavior and emotions.

It's not just about becoming more observant, though. Remember those arguments where words would fly out of your mouth before you actually thought about them? Mindfulness won't eliminate them, you're still human, after all, but they're fewer and farther between. There's often a pause—a small but significant moment where you can choose how to respond rather than just reacting on autopilot.

And it's not just noticing these changes. You can become more present and more engaged in conversations. Then you will recognize when you're falling into old patterns or when something's triggering your insecurities. You will develop a new layer of self-awareness that helps you navigate your relationship with more grace and understanding.

However, perhaps the most profound change for most people who practice mindfulness is their capacity for empathy. By becoming more aware of your emotional landscape, you can become better at reading and responding to other's emotions. When you ask yourself, *"What's really going on here?"* Instead of jumping to conclusions or taking things personally, you can open a whole new world.

These changes don't happen overnight, and they're not always consistent. There are still days when overthinking will get the better of you or when you react without thinking. But overall, the shift will be remarkable. Mindfulness will give you new tools for building and maintaining our relationship—tools that help you stay grounded in the present moment, respond thoughtfully to challenges, and truly see and appreciate your partner.

Practical Implementations

It's easy to read an article or to listen to a podcast that tells you about the benefits of mindfulness. Integrating it into your life is another thing, especially when your mind feels like running a marathon every waking moment. The difference between knowing about mindfulness and practicing it can appear as immense as the Grand Canyon.

But here's the thing: Mindfulness isn't about perfection. It's about practice. It's about showing up repeatedly, even when your mind is screaming at you to check your phone or rehash that argument from last week.

So, how do you make this work in real life?

- Start small. Those 30-minute meditation sessions? Forget about them, at least for now. Start with just 30 seconds a day, a few times a day. It might not seem like much, but it's about building the habit. It's like going to the gym; you don't start with a three-hour workout. You start with what you can manage consistently.

- Use guides, but don't rely on them forever. Guided meditations can be great training wheels. They give your mind something to focus on besides your thoughts. But don't get too dependent on them. Gradually try to do more on your own. It's like learning to ride a bike - at some point, you've got to take off the training wheels.

- Make it a non-negotiable part of your day. Like when you brush your teeth in the morning. It's become as much a part of my routine as that first cup of coffee. Find a time that works for you and stick to it. Consistency is key.

- Bring mindfulness into everyday activities. This level of attention can be a game-changer. Mindfulness doesn't have to be formal meditation. Try being fully present while washing dishes, or pay attention to the sensation of walking as you move. These moments of mindfulness throughout the day can be just as valuable as a dedicated meditation session.

- Be kind to yourself. Your mind will wander. You will get distracted. You will have days where you perceive you're making no progress. That's all part of the process. The key is understanding when it occurs and quietly guiding your attention back without judgment.

- Keep a mindfulness journal. Many people find it helpful to jot down brief notes after each practice. These notes don't need to be elaborate, just a few words about how it went, any insights you had, or challenges you faced. Over time, this can help you see your progress and identify patterns.

- Find a mindfulness buddy. Having someone to share the journey with can be incredibly motivating. Whether it's your partner, a friend, or someone from a mindfulness group, having that support and accountability can make a big difference.

To start off, here are some free mindfulness meditation apps to check out (at the time of this writing):

Insight Timer

https://insighttimer.com/

Offers over 130,000 free guided meditations covering topics like stress, relationships, and sleep. Features include a meditation timer and community discussions.

Smiling Mind

https://www.smilingmind.com.au/

Developed by psychologists and educators, this app provides mindfulness programs tailored for different age groups, including children and adults. It's entirely free and focuses on improving mental well-being.

UCLA Mindful

https://www.uclahealth.org/ulcamindful/ucla-mindful-app

Developed by the UCLA Mindful Awareness Research Center, this app provides free guided meditations and a weekly podcast. It's designed to make mindfulness accessible to everyone.

Mindfulness in Relationship Contexts

Mindfulness is learning to pay more attention, to observe the subtle shifts in your partner's tone, the fleeting expressions that cross their face, and how their body tenses or relaxes in response to your words. It's about sensing the unspoken emotions in your interactions, the things often unsaid but profoundly resonating. It's about becoming acutely aware of your internal landscape, too. It's recognizing the knee-jerk reactions that bubble up inside you, the assumptions that flit through your mind, and the judgments you're tempted to make before your partner has even finished speaking.

This noticing, this heightened awareness, changes the game in relationships. Here's how:

- **You start to listen.** Not the listening where you're just waiting for your turn to speak or formulating your rebuttal in your head. But real, deep listening. You're fully present, absorbing not just the words but the emotion behind them, the context, the nuances. You're noticing the whole person before you, not just the words coming out of their mouth.

- **You create space between stimulus and response.** When your partner says something that would typically set you off, you notice that initial surge of emotion. But instead of immediately reacting, you pause. You become aware that your heart is racing, your clenched jaw. In that pause, that moment of noticing, you can choose your response rather than being at the mercy of your knee-jerk reaction.

- **You tune into your body.** Emotions aren't just mental experiences; they're physical, too. You gain valuable information about your emotional state by noticing the sensations in your body during emotional moments—the tightness in your chest and the butterflies in your stomach. This bodily awareness can be an early warning system, helping you recognize and manage your emotions before they escalate.

- **You observe without judgment.** This is perhaps the trickiest part but also the most transformative. It's about noticing your thoughts and feelings without immediately labeling them as good or bad, right or wrong. It's seeing your partner's actions or words for what they are without immediately overlaying them with your interpretations or assumptions.

This practice of noticing, of bringing mindfulness into your relationship, is not about achieving perfection. It's not about never having conflicts with your partner. We aim to develop those small moments of presence amid our busy, thought-filled lives. It's about learning to be here, even when 'here' is uncomfortable and 'now' is challenging.

When you become an observer in your relationship, you're less likely to get caught up in misunderstandings. You're more likely to catch potential conflicts before they escalate. You will be better equipped to understand your partner's perspective and communicate your needs and feelings.

Mindful Listening

On a train, while on holiday in Berlin, Anne sat behind an old couple, and yes, she was eavesdropping. It wasn't intentional at first, but their interaction was captivating. They weren't discussing anything particularly profound—just their evening dinner plans. But it was how they spoke to each other that caught her attention.

The man spoke slowly, his voice gravelly with age, and the woman leaned in slightly, her eyes fixed on his face. When he paused, searching for a word, she waited patiently, not rushing to fill the silence. When he finished, she asked a question, not to challenge but to understand better. "So you'd prefer the Italian place on the corner, not the one by the river?" she clarified. He nodded, and she smiled, reaching out to pat his hand. Their interaction wasn't grand or dramatic, but something in their quiet exchange felt rare and valuable.

But what does mindful listening really entail? Here are some key aspects:

- **Being fully present means setting aside external distractions** (like phones or TV) and internal (our thoughts and judgments). It's about creating a mental space where your partner's words can truly land.

- **Observing non-verbal cues:** So much of communication is non-verbal. We can gain deeper insights into our partner's emotions and thoughts by paying attention to body language, tone of voice, and facial expressions.

- **Asking clarifying questions:** The woman's simple question about restaurant preference showed her commitment to understanding her husband's perspective. Asking thoughtful questions shows we're interested, and it encourages our partners to express themselves more fully.

- **Creating a conducive environment:** The couple on the train chose a time and place to talk without interruption. It's essential to carve out dedicated time and space for meaningful conversations in our busy lives.

- **Practicing active listening:** Summarize what you've heard to ensure understanding. It's not about parroting back words but reflecting the essence of what's been said.

- **Balancing the conversation:** Mindful listening requires one person talking and the other listening.

The goal of building up that level of attentive, mindful communication is something to strive for in all our relationships. It's not always easy—our minds can be noisy places full of our thoughts, judgments, and distractions. But with practice and intention, we can cultivate this skill.

Okay, so this is what I want you to do now: For a moment, listen, really listen. What do you hear?

Take a full minute—set a timer if you like—and focus on the sounds around you. Don't try to identify or label them; notice them: the distant hum of traffic, perhaps, the whirr of a fan, or even the sound of your breath.

As you listen, you might notice your mind wandering. That's normal. When you catch your thoughts drifting, gently bring your attention to the sounds.

Now, ask yourself:

- How many different sounds did you notice?
- Were there any sounds you hadn't been aware of before this exercise?
- What was it like to concentrate entirely on listening?
- Did you find it easy or challenging to keep your mind from wandering?

This simple exercise is a microcosm of mindful listening in relationships. It's about being present, noticing without judging, and gently refocusing when your mind wanders.

The next time you're conversing with your partner, try to bring this same quality of attention to their words. Listen not just to the content but to the tone, the pauses, the subtle inflections. Notice how it feels to give them your full attention.

A Guided Meditation

Find a quiet, relaxing place; it doesn't matter what time. Maybe you're reading this in your favorite chair, at your kitchen table, or on your morning commute. Wherever you are, let's create a pocket of stillness together.

Take a deep breath. Not the shallow kind that barely moves your chest, but the kind that makes your belly rise like bread dough, the kind that fills all the empty spaces.

Notice the weight of your body where it meets the chair, the floor, and the earth. Feel your feet on the floor and your back against the seat.

Now, about those thoughts racing through your mind—you know the ones—the endless loop of what-ifs and should-haves. We're not going to fight them. Instead, imagine you're sitting by a window on a rainy day. Each thought is just another raindrop sliding down the glass. Some fast, some slow, some merging with others, but all eventually go down and out of sight.

You don't need to wipe the glass clean. Just watch the droplets make their paths.

When a particularly sticky thought comes—maybe about that conversation you need to have with your partner or that decision you've been turning over and over—let it be another raindrop. Watch how it moves, catches the light, and eventually slides away like all the others.

Stay here as long as you like, watching your thought raindrops trace their delicate patterns across the glass.

By doing this, you can grasp the essence of being present. Not empty-minded, not perfectly peaceful, but awake to the moment in all its imperfect beauty.

Your overthinking mind isn't your enemy. It's more like an overeager guard dog doing its best to protect you, even when barking at shadows. Perhaps true mindfulness isn't about silencing this vigilant part of yourself but about learning to pat it on the head and say, "Thank you for trying to keep me safe. I can take it from here."

Mindfulness holds space for both the chaos and the quiet of your mind. You are not the weather of your thoughts—you're the sky that holds both storms and sunshine. Sometimes, the most mindful thing you can do is notice how hard your mind works to keep you safe and love it, anyway.

Chapter Four

Building Effective Communication Skills

Effective communication in practice and what it sounds like when we're able to express our needs, feelings, and boundaries clearly and respectfully sounds like this. "No, I'm not prepared to discuss that now. "It makes me uneasy when you ignore me during our conversations. "I want us to talk about our emotional well-being." "This is my boundary, and I'd like you to respect that." But let's be honest—how often do we communicate like this in our relationships?

These clear, assertive statements seem unfamiliar when spoken for most of us. They stick in our throats, tangled up with fears of conflict, rejection, or appearing too demanding. Instead, we often default to silence, passive-aggression, or explosive outbursts that leave both parties feeling hurt and misunderstood.

Here's the thing about relationship communication: we're all fumbling through it. There's no magical formula, no perfect set of words that will solve every problem. It's messy, uncomfortable, and sometimes downright terrifying, but also necessary. Because without it, we're just two people sharing a space, not a life.

In the following pages, we'll dive into this mess together. We'll talk about why it's so damn hard to say what we mean sometimes. We'll look at how we trip ourselves up, the defenses we throw up, the fears that keep us silent when we should speak.

Working on these skills isn't about becoming some idealized version of a "good communicator." It's about finding our voices in our relationships. It's about learning to listen, even when every fiber of our being wants to interrupt, defend, or shut down.

Will it be comfortable? Probably not. Will it be worth it? Absolutely.

Power Dynamics in Non-Verbal Communication

Sometimes, without realizing it, we engage in subtle power plays through our body language. The way we take up space during an argument, how we position ourselves when having tough conversations, even the height difference between us and our partner—these physical dynamics carry messages about power, control, and equality in our relationships.

Think about it: When feeling defensive, you might cross your arms and lean back, creating physical distance. When trying to assert yourself, you might stand taller and take up more space. In moments of vulnerability, you might shrink and lower your gaze. Most of the time, these aren't conscious choices—they're deeply ingrained responses that reflect and reinforce power dynamics in our relationships.

You might notice this during family gatherings, such as how certain relatives physically position themselves in doorways while speaking, subtly controlling both the conversation and the space. How others make themselves smaller, stepping aside, looking down. These weren't just random movements—they were a physical language of power passed down through generations.

Physical Positioning in Conversations

Awareness of how we position ourselves during difficult conversations will transform your conversations, even arguments. Watch any couple in the middle of a disagreement. Notice how one might lean forward, dominating the space, while the other instinctively backs away. Or how, during serious conversations, one partner might remain standing while the other sits—creating an immediate power imbalance through height difference alone.

These physical dynamics play out in subtler ways, too. It shows up in who walks ahead and who follows behind. Who sits at the head of the table during family dinners. Who stands in front and stays in the back during social gatherings? And even in bed, depending on who takes up more space and who edges toward the corner.

We consciously choose to adjust when we catch ourselves falling into these patterns. We'll both sit down, creating equal ground. We'll step away from walls and corners, ensuring we have space to move freely. Sometimes, it's as simple as facing each other fully instead of having conversations in passing or over shoulders. These minor adjustments in how we physically show up for hard conversations have created a foundation where we are understood, respected, and equally powerful in expressing our needs.

The Height Factor

In most relationships, one partner is usually taller than the other. It's such a familiar dynamic that we rarely consider how it influences our interactions. Until you notice it, the taller partner might unconsciously straighten their spine during arguments, maximizing their height advantage. The shorter partner tilts their head back to maintain eye contact.

Judge and Cable's (2004) research in the Journal of Applied Psychology suggested that height differences affect communication dynamics. Taller partners might unconsciously use their height to emphasize points during arguments. In comparison, shorter partners might need to compensate by speaking louder, gesturing more, or choosing higher ground during conversations.

Our physical stature can unconsciously affect how we communicate and assert ourselves. A taller person might naturally adopt a more dominant stance without realizing it, while their partner might develop subtle compensatory behaviors over time.

I see this play out in my friend's relationship—she's nearly a foot shorter than her husband. During disagreements, she'll often position herself on the stairs or move conversations to where she can sit on the kitchen counter, instinctively seeking equal eye level. He has learned to sit down during serious discussions, a conscious choice to neutralize the height advantage he didn't ask for but naturally possesses.

Control of Space

Consider the subtle ways we claim territory in shared spaces. Who spreads their belongings across shared surfaces? Whose preferences dictate the temperature of the room? Who claims the more comfortable spot on the couch by default?

These seemingly minor spatial decisions reflect deeper patterns of power in relationships. The partner who consistently yields space might also yield voice in other areas of the relationship.

Creating Balance Through Awareness

The key lies in the consciousness of these patterns. Once you notice them, you can make deliberate choices about:

- Moving important conversations to neutral spaces where both partners can sit at eye level.

- Being mindful of not using physical presence to intimidate or dominate.

- Creating environments that allow both partners equal claim to space and comfort.

- Recognizing when physical positioning might influence the dynamic of your interactions.

Beyond Physical Space

Ever notice how specific patterns in your relationship just happened? How are roles and dynamics settled into place without any conscious decision? These unspoken arrangements shape our relationships in ways we rarely examine, creating invisible rules about who does what, who leads where, and who yields when.

The beauty of becoming aware of these patterns lies in the choice it gives us. Once we see them, we can decide if they serve us or need gentle adjustment. Let's explore some of these subtle dynamics in your relationship:

Take a moment to reflect on the subtle power dynamics in your relationship. Reflect on these questions, and if you are willing, talk about them with your partner:

In Your Daily Interactions:

- Who speaks first in group settings?

- Who takes the lead when meeting new people?

- Whose schedule typically determines shared plans?

- Who apologizes more frequently?

In Emotional Expression:

- Who has more freedom to express anger or frustration?
- Who needs to "calm down" more often?
- Whose emotions tend to set the tone for the day?

In Physical Space:

- Who initiates physical affection most often?
- Who decides when physical intimacy ends?
- Who claims the preferred spot on the couch?
- Who adjusts their walking pace to match the other?

In Social Settings:

- Who decides when to leave social gatherings?
- Who speaks for the relationship in group settings?
- Who defers to whom when telling shared stories?
- Who maintains the social calendar?

There are no right or wrong answers here. The goal isn't to achieve perfect equality in every aspect—that's neither realistic nor necessary. Instead, notice these patterns with curiosity rather than judgment. What do they tell you about your relationship's power dynamics? Which patterns would you like to maintain? Which might benefit from gentle adjustment?

Express Needs Effectively With 'I' Statements

We often think of communication as this big, complex thing. We read books, go to therapy, and try to learn all these techniques. But sometimes, it's as simple—and complicated—as saying "I am." When we say "I am," we're simply stating our truth, and there's a power in that, a power that can transform conversations and relationships.

Think about it. How different does "I am feeling ignored" sound compared to "You never pay attention to me"? The first invites understanding, and the second invites defense. The first is about you, your feelings, your experience. The second is an attack, whether you mean it or not.

When we use "I statements," we connect with our feelings and needs and take responsibility for our emotional landscape. Yes, sometimes, it feels safer to hide behind accusations or silence. Sometimes, admitting "I am scared" or "I am hurt" feels like exposing a raw nerve, but real intimacy exists in that vulnerability, that honesty.

And it goes beyond just expressing feelings. "I am" statements can also be powerful tools for expressing needs. "I need some alone time." "I am hoping for more physical affection." These statements put our needs out there, unambiguous, without demanding or blaming. In your next conversation with your partner, pay attention to your words. How often do you say "You always" or "You never"? How might those statements change if you started with "I am" instead? I hope this small change can make a big difference in your relationship. I am excited for you to discover the power of your voice and truth.

What are you? What do you need? Are you ready to say it?

Recognizing and Responding to Non-Verbal Cues

The body says more than what the mouth does. It's an old wisdom that holds profound truth in our daily interactions, especially in our closest relationships. Our bodies constantly speak, sending out signals we may not be aware of. A raised eyebrow, a slight lean forward, a tightening of the jaw—these subtle movements can speak volumes, often louder than our words.

The Basics of Non-Verbal Communication

Non-verbal communication consists of gestures, expressions, and postures that convey messages without words. We all use these signals, often unconsciously. For example:

- Crossed arms might indicate discomfort or defensiveness.
- An open stance could suggest openness to interaction.
- A smile doesn't always signify happiness; it might mask discomfort or anxiety.

Understanding teaches you to become more aware of the subtle signals in your interactions. This awareness helps you gauge the emotional state of others and respond appropriately.

Key aspects to observe include facial expressions, posture, gestures, eye contact (or lack thereof), and tone of voice. By paying attention to these elements, we can often get a clearer picture of what someone is communicating beyond their words.

Cultural Differences in Non-Verbal Communication

Megan visited Japan a few years back and met a local businessman for coffee. As she sat down, she extended her hand for a handshake, only to be met with a bow. At that moment, she realized how deeply ingrained our non-verbal habits are and how easily they can lead to misunderstandings across cultures.

This experience highlighted a crucial aspect of non-verbal communication: it's not universal. What's considered polite or respectful in one culture might be seen as rude or inappropriate in another. For example:

1. **Eye contact:**

    - In many Western cultures, direct eye contact is seen as a sign of attentiveness and honesty.

    - In some Asian and Middle Eastern cultures, prolonged eye contact can be perceived as disrespectful or confrontational.

2. **Personal space:**

    - North Americans and Northern Europeans generally prefer more personal space in conversations.

    - In Latin American and Middle Eastern cultures, closer proximity is often the norm and can signify warmth and engagement.

3. **Gestures:**

    - The 'thumbs up' gesture is positive in many Western countries but can be offensive in parts of the Middle East and West Africa.

    - Nodding the head may mean 'yes' in most cultures, but in Bulgaria and Greece, it typically means 'no.'

4. **Touch:**

    - In some Mediterranean and Middle Eastern cultures, same-sex friends may hold hands as a sign of friendship.

    - In many Asian cultures, touching someone you've just met, even for a handshake, can be uncomfortable.

5. **Facial expressions:**

    - While smiling is generally seen as positive, in some Asian cultures, smiling can be used to mask negative emotions or discomfort.

These cultural differences complicate our interactions, especially in our globalized world. They remind us that there's no one-size-fits-all approach to understanding non-verbal cues.

To navigate these differences effectively:

- **Research:** Research their communication norms before interacting with people from different cultural backgrounds.

- **Observe:** Pay attention to how others interact within their cultural context.

- **Ask:** If you're unsure about a non-verbal cue, asking for clarification is okay.

- **Be flexible**: Be willing to adapt your non-verbal communication style when necessary.

- **Don't assume:** Avoid jumping to conclusions based on your cultural norms.

You don't have to become an expert in every culture's non-verbal language, just develop enough awareness, show respect, and be open to learning. This approach not only helps avoid misunderstandings but can also lead to richer, more meaningful cross-cultural interactions. If you are in a multi-cultural relationship or maybe your in-laws are much more embedded in their culture than your partner, by not being savvy to these differences it may still cause communication issues in your relationship.

The Feedback Loop: A Two-Way Street

Communication isn't just about sending messages; it's about receiving them, too. Our non-verbal responses create a feedback loop, constantly shaping and reshaping the conversation. A nod, a smile, a furrowed brow—these reactions can encourage, discourage, or redirect the flow of dialogue.

Awareness of this feedback loop isn't just about reading others; it's about becoming more conscious of our non-verbal signals. Are we listening, or are our bodies betraying disinterest? Are we inviting open dialogue, or are we unconsciously shutting it down?

Mindfulness: The Key to Deeper Understanding

We discussed mindfulness in Chapter 3. Let's delve a little deeper in how this can help us with deeper understanding. Often associated with meditation and stress relief, mindfulness plays a crucial role in non-verbal communication. It's about sharpening our awareness to catch subtle, unnoticed cues. In relationships, mindful communication can transform how we interact and understand each other.

When we practice mindful communication, we create space for deeper understanding. Instead of jumping to conclusions based on a furrowed brow or crossed arms, we pause to consider what these signals might mean in the context of our interaction.

Mindfulness also helps us become aware of our non-verbal cues. Are your shoulders tense? Is your breathing shallow? Are you leaning in or pulling away? Recognizing these physical signals in ourselves makes us better at noticing them in others.

To incorporate mindfulness into your communication, try these practical exercises:

- The Three-Breath Practice: Take three deep breaths to center yourself before a meaningful conversation.

- Body Scan: Regularly check in with your body during interactions, noticing areas of tension or relaxation.

- Curiosity Cultivator: When you notice something in your partner's non-verbal communication, get curious instead of assuming.

By approaching our interactions with mindfulness, we open up new possibilities:

- We become better listeners, picking up on unspoken messages.

- We respond more thoughtfully, avoiding knee-jerk reactions.

- We build stronger bonds when others acknowledge and understand our presence.

- We navigate conflicts more skillfully, recognizing tensions early.

We must teach ourselves this practice and return to it repeatedly. It makes us more empathetic, understanding, and connected in our relationships.

Where do I start if I want to become better at interpreting what people mean without words? It's not like I can enroll in "Body Language 101" at the local community college. Improving our non-verbal communication skills is a lot like learning a new language—it takes practice, patience, and a willingness to make mistakes.

Here's a week-long challenge to kick-start your non-verbal communication journey:

Day 1: Become an observer: Spend one day watching people. Not in a creepy way, mind you, but pay attention to how people carry themselves, their facial expressions, and their gestures. Don't try to interpret yet. Just observe.

Day 2: Learn how to mirror: Try mirroring your partner's body language during a conversation. If they lean in, you lean in. If they cross their arms, you cross yours. Notice how this affects your perception of the interaction.

Day 3: Notice your body: Do quick body scans of yourself throughout the day. Are your shoulders tense? Jaw clenched? Awareness of your non-verbal cues is the first step to managing them.

Day 4: Challenge assumptions: When making an assumption based on someone's non-verbal cues, challenge it. Instead of thinking, "They must be angry," ask yourself, "What else could this mean?"

Day 5: Become curious: Ask open-ended questions about what you observe. "I noticed you got quiet when I mentioned the party. What's on your mind?"

Day 6: The Cultural Explorer: Research non-verbal cues in a different culture. How does this new knowledge change your perspective on communication?

Day 7: The Honest Reflection: Have an open conversation about non-verbal communication in your relationship with your partner. What cues do you pick up from each other? What often gets misinterpreted?

Notice the sighs, the smiles, the subtle shifts in posture. Be curious to ask, "Hey, what's going on?" when something seems off. Will you mess up? Absolutely. You'll misread signals, you'll jump to conclusions, you'll probably make an ass of yourself more than once. That's how we learn, right?

Words carry worlds within them. Every "I hear you," every "I'm sorry," and every "help me understand" opens a door between two people. Between what we mean and what we say lies the work of actual communication—not in crafting perfect sentences, but in showing up with an honest heart and the willingness to try again when our words fall short.

Sometimes, the most potent communication happens in the spaces between our words—in the pause before responding, in the gentle tone that carries care, in the courage to stay present when silence feels heavy. More than any practiced phrase or perfect response, these moments tell our partners that their voice matters, that their feelings have a home with us, and that we choose to understand even when understanding takes work.

Chapter Five

Overcoming Relationship Anxiety

For so many, the 'what ifs' can be deafening, casting shadows over even the most cherished relationships. Do you find these questions swirling around in your head?

"What if I choose the wrong spouse and I end up with this crippling anxiety for the rest of my life?"

"What if I don't actually love my partner, and I'm just gaslighting myself into thinking that I do because I idolize marriage and am just tired of waiting around for a partner?"

"Was that post I just saw a sign that I should leave this relationship?"

What if... what if... what if...

These thoughts are exhausting and relentless, stealing the joy right out of your relationship.

If you care too much about a person, obsessing yourself to the bone won't take away the grief or the fear that resides in that place that reminds us that we might lose them.

Let's be clear: Relationship anxiety isn't some cute quirk or a sign that you care too much, and it's not reasonable. Anyone who promises that is selling you snake oil. Let's discover a way to understand where these anxieties come from and how to manage them so they don't ruin your life—or your relationship.

We'll look at the roots of relationship anxiety, how it manifests, and why it's so damn persistent. We'll explore strategies that work, not just empty promises or quick fixes. And yes, we'll talk about when to bring in professional help because sometimes, we need more than a book can offer.

We will learn to find ways to be present and connect, even when your brain is shouting at you to run and hide. I want to teach you how to build a relationship that's strong enough to weather the storms of anxiety.

Identify the Roots of Relationship-Related Anxieties

Jan's grandmother was a storyteller, and she used to tell us that roots are the most important part of any plant. "You can't see them," she'd say, her eyes twinkling, "but they determine how strong the plant will grow, how well it will weather the storms." She'd pause, letting the words sink in, before adding, "And it's the same with people, my dears. Our roots shape who we become."

She remembers sitting in her garden as a child, surrounded by a profusion of colors and scents. She'd point to the towering oak at the edge of the property, its branches reaching far into the sky. "That tree," she'd say, "has roots that go deeper than you can imagine. That's why it stands tall and survives drought and wind."

Then she'd gesture to a nearby rosebush, its blossoms vibrant but its stem bent. "This one," she'd explain, "wasn't planted deep enough. Its roots are shallow. It's beautiful, but it struggles when the weather turns harsh."

At the time, Jan thought she was talking about gardening. It wasn't until years later, when Jan grappled with her relationship anxieties, that she truly understood what her grandmother meant.

Our anxieties, like plants, have roots. Hidden, often tangled, and sometimes painful to unearth. But understanding these roots is crucial if we want to grow beyond them. Like that bent rosebush, if our emotional roots are shallow or damaged, we might struggle when our relationships face challenges. We might find ourselves easily shaken by doubts, quickly assuming the worst, or constantly seeking reassurance.

If we can dig deep, understand the roots of our anxieties, and nurture our emotional soil, we can grow strong—like an old, steadfast oak.

Jan's grandmother's garden taught me that it takes time, patience, and sometimes a willingness to get our hands dirty as we dig through the layers of our past. But it also taught me that with understanding and care, even the most anxious hearts can learn to stand tall and weather the storms of life.

Early Attachment Styles and Family Dynamics

Our childhood experiences lay the foundation for adult relationships, shaping how we connect with others and perceive love and security. How our caregivers interact with us establishes patterns that often persist long into adulthood, influencing our expectations and behaviors in intimate relationships.

We touched on attachment theories in Chapter 1. Now let's dive a little deeper to find their roots. Attachment theory, developed by psychologist John Bowlby, identifies several attachment styles that develop in childhood:

Secure Attachment: When caregivers are consistently responsive and tuned to a child's needs, the child develops a secure attachment. These individuals often grow into adults comfortable with intimacy and independence in relationships.

Formation of a secure attachment with an infant is all about offering care that is consistent, responsive, and nurturing—care that makes the infant feel safe and valued. Here are the principal practices for ensuring that an infant forms a secure attachment. I'm not sure many of us had this type of nurturing, but I add the information here so that we can do better and help others do better. Even if you didn't experience secure attachment as an infant, there's hope. You can still develop the tools and strategies to build secure, fulfilling relationships today.

It is vital to attend to the baby's cries, coos, and other body language signals. The baby needs to learn that their communication elicits a prompt, soothing response from you. When you tend to the essential signals your baby gives off, they will learn that they are understood and safe, leading to a secure attachment.

Anxious Attachment: If a caregiver is inconsistent in their responsiveness, alternating between attentive and neglectful, a child might develop an anxious attachment style. As adults, these individuals often fear abandonment and seek constant reassurance from their partners.

Avoidant Attachment: Children may develop an avoidant attachment style when caregivers are consistently unresponsive or dismissive. In adulthood, this can manifest as discomfort with closeness and a tendency to distance themselves in relationships emotionally.

Disorganized Attachment: This style can develop when caregivers are a source of both comfort and fear, perhaps because of abuse or unresolved trauma. Adults with this attachment style may have chaotic relationships, struggling with trust, and emotional regulation.

These early experiences shape our internal working models of relationships. For instance, a child with an anxious attachment might internalize the belief that love is unreliable and that they must constantly strive to keep their caregiver's attention. As an adult, this could translate into:

- Hypervigilance to signs of rejection or abandonment.
- Intense anxiety when a partner is not immediately responsive.
- A tendency to seek excessive reassurance about a partner's feelings.
- Difficulty trusting in the stability of relationships.

Family dynamics also play a crucial role. The relationships we observe between our parents or other significant family members serve as our first models of adult relationships. A child who witnesses volatile arguments might grow up to view conflict as threatening or usual, affecting how they handle disagreements in their relationships.

Cultural factors intersect with these experiences as well. In some cultures, close family ties and interdependence are valued concepts, while others prioritize independence. These cultural norms can influence attachment styles and relationship expectations.

As adults, these early experiences can translate into doubts about our partner's love or commitment, even when these fears are unfounded. Someone with an anxious attachment style might interpret a partner's need for alone time as a sign of waning interest, triggering intense anxiety. An individual with an avoidant attachment might see everyday expressions of affection as suffocating, causing them to retreat and pressure the relationship.

Recognizing these early attachment patterns is crucial in addressing current relationship anxieties, allowing us to:

1. Recognize the source of our emotional responses.
2. Differentiate between past wounds and present realities.
3. Communicate our needs more effectively to our partners.

4. Work towards developing more secure attachment patterns.

While our early experiences shape us, they don't define us. Developing more secure attachment styles and healthier relationship patterns is possible with awareness and effort. To do this involves self-reflection, therapy, or consciously practicing new ways of relating to partners.

Patterns in Past Relationships

What did your last relationship teach you? Think about it for a moment and let the memories surface. Was it the way your heart raced when they didn't text back for hours? Or maybe how you always seemed to pick fights over the most minor things? These aren't just random occurrences—they're clues, breadcrumbs leading us back to the source of our relationship anxieties.

Our past relationships reflect our deepest fears and insecurities. They show us how we love and react when that love feels threatened and essentially what helps us differentiate between our triggers and our partners' behaviors.

Here are some questions that I want you to think about:

- In your past relationships, did you find yourself constantly seeking reassurance? You might have sought daily declarations of affection to achieve peace of mind.

- Did conflicts send you into a spiral of worst-case scenarios? Perhaps a simple disagreement had you convinced the relationship was doomed.

- How did you react when your partner needed space? Did you respect their boundaries, or did it trigger feelings of abandonment?

- Were there patterns in the type of partners you chose? Maybe you consistently found yourself drawn to emotionally unavailable people.

Suppose you notice that specific reactions or feelings occur regardless of who your partner is. In that case, you're likely looking at a personal trigger, so these anxieties and insecurities you bring into every relationship, shaped by your experiences and attachment style.

For example, if in every relationship you've had, you've felt intense jealousy when your partner spends time with friends, that's probably more about your insecurities than your partner's behavior. Or if you've always struggled to express your needs, fearing that doing so would drive your partner away, that's a pattern you're carrying with you.

On the other hand, if you find that your anxiety was explicitly triggered by a particular partner's behavior—like consistent lying or emotional manipulation—that's different. Those are valid responses to problematic behavior, not necessarily reflecting your issues. It would help if you didn't shift all blame, but try to understand where your anxieties come from so that you can start to address them more effectively.

Irrational Thought Patterns

If our brains had an on and off button, the first thing that would benefit us all is to switch off that voice that always assumes the worst. You know the one—the voice that turns a simple "I'm running late" text into a full-blown relationship crisis. The thing with our brains is that they're always on high alert for potential threats, and in relationships, this hypervigilance often manifests as irrational thought patterns, so basically:

Catastrophizing is your brain's disaster movie channel. Your partner doesn't answer their phone, and suddenly, you're convinced they're lying in a ditch somewhere or, worse, they've decided they don't love you anymore. It's exhausting.

Black-and-white thinking is where there is no room for nuance in this mindset. Either your relationship is perfect, or it's doomed. Your partner is either madly in love with you or secretly plotting their escape. Reality, of course, is usually somewhere in the messy middle.

Mind reading is when you're confident you know what your partner is thinking, usually something negative. "They didn't compliment my new haircut, so they must not find me attractive anymore."

Overgeneralization is when one argument becomes, "We always fight." One forgotten anniversary turns into "You never remember anything important."

Thoughts like these distort our perception of reality and turn small things into unnecessarily big things, but the light at the end of the tunnel is that once you can identify these distortions, you can start challenging them.

Try this: The next time you catch yourself spiraling into one of these thought patterns, pause. Take a deep breath. Then ask yourself:

- Is there any actual evidence for this thought?

- What would I tell a friend if they were having this thought?

- Are there other possible explanations for this situation?

For instance, if your partner's text replies are slower than usual, instead of jumping to "They're losing interest in me," consider other possibilities. Maybe they're swamped at work, their phone battery died, or they're driving and being responsible for not texting.

Challenging these irrational thoughts isn't about forcing positivity. It's about striving for a more balanced, realistic perspective. It's about training your brain to consider multiple possibilities rather than defaulting to the worst-case scenario. Thoughts are not facts; they're merely stories that your brain tells you, and sometimes, those stories need a good edit.

Fostering Open Dialogue

The greatest blessing is when we can muster enough courage to speak our truth and lay our hearts bare before our partners. In these moments of vulnerability, we truly connect and bridge the gap between our inner worlds and theirs.

But let's be honest—finding that courage isn't always easy. How many times have you bitten your tongue and swallowed your feelings, all to keep the peace? How often have you lain awake at night, your mind buzzing with unspoken words?

Open communication is more than just talking. It's about building a bond where both individuals have the security to be completely authentic, with all their imperfections. It's about constructing a foundation strong enough to hold your dreams, joys, fears, and insecurities.

Imagine a relationship where you don't have to guess what your partner is thinking, where you don't have to walk on eggshells around specific topics. Sounds liberating.

Here's how you can start fostering this kind of openness:

- Make it clear that your relationship is a safe space for sharing. This means no eye-rolling, no dismissive comments, no matter how trivial the concern might seem.

- When your partner is speaking, really listen. Please put down your phone, turn off the TV, and give them your full attention. Show them that their words matter to you.

- You don't need formal meetings with agendas. It's about setting aside time to connect when you're both relaxed. Maybe it's over Sunday morning coffee or during an evening walk.

- If diving into deep conversations feels daunting, start with smaller shares. Talk about your day, thoughts on a book you're reading, or a dream. Build up to the bigger stuff.

- If something's bothering you, say so. Don't expect your partner to be a mind reader. And when you do share, use "I" statements to express your feelings without blaming.

- When your partner shares something difficult, thank them for trusting you. This encouragement can make them more comfortable opening up in the future.

Communication doesn't have to be perfect. It needs to be a space where both of you are comfortable enough to be genuine and share your truths, even if they are messy or complicated.

Establishing Conflict Handling Agreements

Jan and Tim have this thing that they do on Sunday afternoons. It started by accident. They were sitting on their worn leather couch, mugs of coffee cooling on the side table, when they stumbled into a conversation about the week's frustrations. Not the big stuff, mind you, but the little things—the unwashed dishes, the forgotten errands, the misplaced keys.

At first, it felt awkward, like they were airing our dirty laundry in the warm Sunday light. But as they talked, something shifted. The frustrations became less about blame and more about understanding. They weren't just complaining; they were problem-solving together.

Now, it's become a ritual. Every Sunday, they carve out an hour or so. Sometimes, on that same couch or walking in the park. But wherever they are, they are creating a space to figure out how to love each other better and be honest and vulnerable.

This is called "relationship maintenance" time. It sounds clinical, but it can feel like anything but-care, intention, or choosing each other over and over again.

These conversations are not always easy—sometimes, they might involve tears, frustration, or the realization that there has been unintentional hurt. Maybe your relationship maintenance looks different. A quiet walk in the park or a shared hobby brings you joy. Regardless of its appearance, the essential point is building a space for honest and uninhibited communication. Here are some ideas to help you establish your conflict-handling agreements:

- Agree on a phrase or gesture you can call a time-out during heated moments. It could be as simple as saying, "Let's take five," or a hand signal you both understand. Don't avoid the issue; give yourself space to cool down and think clearly.

- Take turns sitting in a designated "listening chair" where your only job is to listen without interrupting. When it's your turn to listen, focus on understanding, not formulating your response.

- Start difficult conversations by expressing feelings rather than accusations. "It pains me when..." often goes over better than "You always..."

- After one person speaks, the other tries to replay what they heard, ensuring you're both on the same page. It may seem strange initially, but it can prevent many misunderstandings.

- When discussing problems, focus more on what you'd like in the future rather than dwelling on past mistakes. It's about progress, not punishment.

When bringing up issues, start and end with something you appreciate about your partner. It helps keep things in perspective and reminds you why you're putting in this effort.

Building Trust in Challenging Situations

Saying "I trust you" can look like many different things. For one, it can look like a couple fumbling through their first attempt at assembling IKEA furniture. It might be a disaster of misaligned boards and mysteriously "extra" screws, punctuated by frustrated sighs and nervous laughter.

But in that chaos, maybe you find a rhythm. Learning to hand each other tools without asking, to step back when the other needed space, and to laugh at mistakes instead of blaming them. That wordless dance of cooperation? That's trust in action.

Yes, it's also about finding consistency in the small things. The good morning text arrives consistently, even on the busiest days; it's remembering exactly how your partner takes their coffee and has it ready for them. In long-distance relationships, the video call happens, rain or shine. These seemingly minor acts of reliability build a foundation of security. They whisper, "You can count on me," in a world that sometimes feels unpredictable.

However, in its most magnificent way, it looks a lot like vulnerability: opening up about your fears, your insecurities, your dreams, and even when your instincts scream at you to keep your walls up. It's admitting, "I'm terrified of meeting your parents," or "I'm struggling with jealousy, and I don't know why."

This kind of openness is terrifying, but it's also an invitation. It allows your partner to step in, offer support, and say, "I've got you." We create a shared emotional space by sharing our true selves, fears, and all. We transform individual worries into challenges we face together, strengthening our bond.

Your anxious heart isn't trying to sabotage your love story; it's trying to write one where you never get hurt again, but love and certainty rarely share the same page. The grace lies not in silencing your fears but in learning to hold them more gently, in understanding that they're part of your story but not the whole story.

Your capacity for love is bigger than your anxiety about it. While your mind spins stories of what could go wrong, your heart still knows how to reach out, trust, and stay. And maybe that's the real victory—not in never feeling afraid, but in choosing to love anyway, in all its beautiful uncertainty.

Building Trust in Your Relationship

Trust is the cornerstone of any strong, lasting relationship. It fosters emotional safety, open communication, and a deeper connection between partners. However, trust doesn't appear overnight; it's built over time through consistent actions, shared experiences, and mutual respect. Here are practical ways to nurture trust in your relationship:

Steps to Build Trust:

Practice Honest Communication-Transparency is key. Share your thoughts, feelings, and intentions openly, even when the conversation is challenging. Honesty builds a foundation of reliability.

Keep Your Promises-Follow through on commitments, big or small. Consistently honoring your word shows your partner that they can rely on you.

Listen Actively-Pay attention to your partner's words without interrupting or judging. This act of active listening is a powerful way to show respect and value your partner's thoughts and feelings.

Show Vulnerability-Sharing your fears, dreams, and insecurities fosters intimacy and signals that you trust your partner with your authentic self.

For instance, you could share a childhood fear or a personal dream that you've been hesitant to talk about.

Apologize and Forgive-Acknowledge when you're wrong, and make amends sincerely. Likewise, be willing to forgive your partner's mistakes to maintain emotional harmony.

Be Consistent-Demonstrate your values and intentions through consistent behavior. Mixed signals can erode trust.

Support Each Other-Be there during tough times and celebrate each other's successes. Knowing you have each other's back reinforces trust.

Respect Boundaries-Honor your partner's personal and emotional boundaries. This means respecting their need for personal space, understanding their emotional triggers, and not pushing them to share more than they're comfortable with. This shows that you value their autonomy and feelings.

Address Issues Directly-Avoiding problems can lead to misunderstandings. Tackle conflicts with a problem-solving mindset and mutual respect. This doesn't mean you should push your partner to discuss something they're not ready to, but that you should be open to addressing issues when they arise.

By practicing these habits, you can create a safe, trusting environment where your relationship can thrive. Trust takes effort, but it brings rewards of deeper connection, lasting love, and a sense of security that can inspire and motivate you in your relationship journey.

Unlock the Power of Generosity

*"Overthinking is like a rocking chair. It gives you something to do but gets you nowhere." — **Glenn Turner***

Many of us know that feeling: replaying conversations, second-guessing what we said, or worrying if our partner is really happy. *The Overthinker's Guide to Relationship Communication aims to help people step out of that spiral and build stronger, more confident connections.*

But here's the thing...we can't reach everyone who needs this book without your help.

Would you help someone you've never met, even if no one ever knew you did?

Who is this person, you ask? They're a lot like you—or like you used to be. Unsure about how to navigate their thoughts, wanting to build better relationships, but not knowing where to start.

Our mission is simple: make relationship communication less stressful and more fulfilling for everyone. And for that mission to succeed, we need to reach as many people as possible.

That's where you come in. Most people do, in fact, judge a book by its cover—and by its reviews. So here's my heartfelt ask:

Would you leave a review for this book?

Your review takes less than 60 seconds to write and doesn't cost a penny, but it could make a world of difference to someone who needs this book. Your words might be the reason they take a step toward healthier communication.

Your review could help:

- ...one more person quiet their overthinking.

- ...one more couple break free from miscommunication.

- ...one more relationship grow stronger and happier.

To give that gift of understanding and connection, all you have to do is leave a review. It's quick, simple, and impactful.

Scan the QR code below or use the link below to share your thoughts.

https://www.amazon.com/review/review-your-purchases/?asin=B0DNNQ5HG7

If you believe this book could help someone else, your review might be the nudge they need.

Thank you sincerely for helping us make relationship communication accessible and empowering. Now, let's dive back into the chapters ahead.

– Your biggest fan, Sage Lifestyle Press

PS – Fun fact: Helping others brings unexpected rewards. If this book helped you, consider sending it to a friend who might need it too.

Chapter Six

Personal Growth and Self-Reflection

In a month, a week, a year, and even two years, you will not be the same person you are today but a happier person having done this work. It's like looking at old photos and barely recognizing yourself. Not because you look so different (though maybe you do), but because you can't quite remember what it felt like to be your old self anymore.

Kris found an old journal from five years ago; reading it was like eavesdropping on a stranger's thoughts. The worries that kept her up at night then seem so trivial now. The dreams she had, some of them have come true, new ones have replaced others she couldn't have imagined back then, and her relationship?

They have been through a dozen different versions of themselves together. There was the "we're invincible" phase when they first fell in love. The "who are you and what have we become" phase when life got tough. The "I'm changing, and I'm terrified you won't like the new me" phase.

Each phase taught them something. Each version of themselves brought something new to the table. Sometimes, it was a gift, sometimes a challenge. Often, it was both. Kris thinks about the fights with her partner—not the petty ones about dishes or schedules, but the deep ones. The ones where they were fighting themselves, their fears and insecurities, and the other person just being caught in the crossfire. Those fights? They're growth in disguise; painful, messy growth, but growth nonetheless.

The quiet moments are growth too; the times when we sit in comfortable silence, each lost in our thoughts but somehow still connected; the times when we share a look and know exactly what the other is thinking, not because we're mind readers, but because we've grown together and created our silent language.

Do you ever wonder, if we could meet our future selves, would we recognize them? Would we like them? Would we be proud of them? Wouldn't it be wonderful if we saw ourselves as a little wiser, kinder, and more comfortable in our skin?

Growth is always pretty, though. It's terrifying, messy, uncomfortable, and many other feelings. It's looking at parts of yourself you've kept hidden and saying, "Okay, let's deal with this." It's admitting when you're wrong, when you're scared, when you need help.

In the following pages, we will talk about this journey, not as experts with all the answers, but as fellow travelers on this winding road of personal growth and relationships. We'll share stories, ask questions, and maybe, just maybe, figure out a few things along the way.

Reflect on Attachment Styles and How They Influence Behavior

After years of doing the inner work and working hard to heal, Shelly realized that her attachment style was a story she'd been telling for years—a story written in invisible ink, influencing every relationship she'd ever had.

One morning, she sat at her kitchen table. Just having experienced another near-argument with her partner, where tension quietly simmered beneath the surface, yet no one voices it aloud. She notices a pattern: In every relationship, romantic or otherwise, she always keeps one foot out of the door, ready to leave at the first sign of trouble. She had long considered it as independence, but it was fear disguised as courage.

That moment challenged her to unpack her attachment style; it felt like opening an old box in the attic full of things I'd forgotten I was carrying around. Memories of her father's long business trips, her mother's anxious hovering, and the time her best friend moved away without saying goodbye were lessons in love and loss that shaped her view of relationships. She recognized that her avoidant attachment style wasn't a life sentence but a default setting that she could change if willing to do the work.

So she began small. The next time she felt the urge to pull away from her partner, she leaned in instead. It felt uncomfortable, like wearing shoes on the wrong feet, but it was also exhilarating, like learning a new language. She reframed the stories she told herself about relationships.

"Everyone leaves eventually" shifted to "Some people might leave, but some also stay, and it's worth the risk." "I don't need anyone," softened to "It's okay to need people sometimes."

There are still days when her old patterns appear like a familiar, cozy sweater she wants to slip back into—but more and more, she finds herself choosing a new path. She is rewriting her attachment story, one small choice at a time.

Working With Your Attachment Style

The first step to understanding your attachment style is noticing your patterns. Maybe you're the person who always keeps their phone on silent, screening calls because emotional closeness feels overwhelming, or perhaps you're checking your messages every five minutes when someone doesn't respond right away, your mind spinning in the worst-case scenarios.

These clues, like signposts, lead us back to our attachment style.

Here's what working with these patterns can look like:

For Anxious Attachment:

Notice when you're in the spiral of seeking reassurance. Before sending that third "Are you okay?" text, pause. Take a breath. Ask yourself: "Is this about the present moment, or am I reacting to old wounds?" Sometimes, just this pause can help break the cycle.

For Avoidant Attachment:

Pay attention to your impulse to pull away. When your partner desires emotional connection, and you experience the familiar desire to pull away, remain present longer than you find comfortable. Not forever—just a few seconds more. It's like building a muscle; it gets stronger with practice.

For Disorganized Attachment:

Track your push-pull patterns. When you feel strongly attracted to someone and are abruptly frightened of them, take heed. Start keeping a simple log of your reactions. What triggered them? What physical sensations did you experience? Understanding these patterns is the first step to changing them.

The key is to make small, consistent shifts, like adjusting the steering wheel slightly when your car drifts—tiny corrections that, over time, keep you on course.

Working with the way you form attachments is your responsibility. It's not about blaming yourself or your past. It's much more about the gentle, persistent steps toward the relationship patterns you want to create.

Growth Through Self-Compassion

Reactions hurt, but responses heal. What is meant by this is that everything leads back to the nervous system. It's science, and it's also the way our bodies carry stories of past hurts, past relationships, and past versions of ourselves. When we react from this wounded place, we often end up causing more pain—to ourselves and others.

Think about the last time you were triggered in your relationship. Maybe your partner took too long to respond to a text, and you were flooded with memories of being ignored, abandoned, and dismissed. Your body tensed, your heart raced, your thoughts spiraled. That's not just anxiety—it's your nervous system running an old program, trying to protect you from past hurts.

Learning is that meeting these moments with judgment only adds another layer of pain. Berating yourself for being "too sensitive" or "too needy" doesn't help or heal; it merely pushes the hurt deeper. Real growth starts with meeting ourselves exactly where we are.

We understand that our reactions, even the messy ones, make perfect sense given our history. With learning to say, "Of course, you're feeling this way. Of course, this is hard. Of course, you're trying to protect yourself."

Where Growth and Self-Compassion Meet

Self-compassion, in theory, is an easy enough concept to digest, but what is difficult is watching yourself spiral into the same relationship pattern for the fifth time this week, catching yourself in behaviors you swore you'd outgrown, or realizing you're still carrying defense mechanisms from your teenage years.

Attachment theory shows that our early relationships, particularly with caregivers, shape how we form connections with others throughout life, and thus these defense mechanisms closely tie to them. If you experienced inconsistent affection or emotional neglect, you might develop an anxious attachment style, leading to behaviors like people-pleasing or seeking constant reassurance in adult relationships. Conversely, if criticism or indifference met your attempts to express emotions, you might develop an avoidant attachment style, using emotional withdrawal or detachment as defense mechanisms.

These patterns, born out of necessity for emotional survival, often become ingrained. You might pull away when intimacy feels too close or over-analyzing a partner's every move, not because of the current situation but as a response to old wounds. Understanding how your attachment style influences these defenses can offer clarity, helping you break free from repeating cycles and move toward more secure, fulfilling relationships.

Personal growth requires us to honestly examine aspects of ourselves. However, it's important to remember that being honest without also being kind to ourselves can lead to self-criticism rather than constructive growth. Shaming yourself won't speed up growth; it will worsen struggles.

Some days, you'll handle a situation with the emotional maturity of a serenity sage. Other days, you'll act from old wounds, playing out scripts you thought you'd burned. Both experiences are part of the journey.

When we wrap our growing edges in compassion, something shifts. We stop treating our patterns like enemies to be defeated and start seeing them as parts of ourselves that need understanding. Understanding ourselves and considering our behaviors isn't about lowering our standards or accepting less from ourselves. It's about creating conditions where genuine change becomes possible.

After all, you can't hate yourself for becoming someone you love.

Balancing Accountability With Kindness

We equate accountability with punishment. We think holding ourselves accountable means berating ourselves for every mistake, replaying our failures on a loop in our minds, and withholding self-compassion until we've somehow "earned" it back.

In its truest form, accountability recognizes where and what we're doing. We examine our progress, recognizing patterns like conflict avoidance, now with awareness.

Real accountability asks questions like:

- What am I doing?
- Who am I becoming?
- How do my actions align with who I want to be?
- What needs attention or change?

But it doesn't stop at questions. It moves into action, into conscious choice. You might notice that you're falling into defensive patterns during arguments. Accountability isn't beating yourself up about this. It's saying, "I see this pattern, I understand why it developed, and I'm choosing to work on it."

Kindness, in this instance, is a part of the equation—not to let ourselves off the hook, but as the foundation that makes real accountability possible. When we're kind to ourselves, we can look at our behaviors more honestly. We don't need to hide from our mistakes or justify our actions. We can see them for what they are and choose differently.

In a nutshell, you can think of it this way: accountability is the compass that shows us where we're headed, and kindness is the steady ground we need under our feet to make the journey. Without it, kindness becomes enablement. Without kindness, accountability becomes punishment. We need both to grow.

The practice looks like this: "I'm falling into old patterns. This makes sense, given my history. Now, how do I want to show up differently?" It holds the understanding of why we do what we do and the aspiration to do better. It's being able to say "I messed up" without adding "because I'm a mess."

With enough balance, we can change how we perceive relationship growth. Instead of swinging between harsh self-criticism and avoidance of responsibility, we find a middle path. A path where we can acknowledge our impact on others while maintaining our dignity and self-respect.

Practical Ways to Maintain Self-Compassion While Working on Relationships

When things seem overwhelming, be they emotions or thoughts that won't leave you alone, remember that you carry more than just the present moment. You carry past hurts, old relationship beliefs, and patterns learned long ago. No wonder it feels overwhelming sometimes.

In these moments, self-compassion isn't just an excellent idea—it's a necessity. Like putting on your oxygen mask first during an emergency, caring for yourself becomes the foundation for all other growth.

Pause when you fall into an old pattern—maybe getting clingy when your partner needs space or pulling away when they reach for connection. Notice the impulse. Then, instead of diving into self-criticism, try treating yourself like you would a friend who's struggling.

Say to yourself, "Of course, this feels hard. Of course, these patterns show up—they helped you survive once. Of course, change takes time."

Growth requires both gentleness and courage, the gentleness to acknowledge where we are without judgment and the courage to keep moving forward, even when it's uncomfortable. It's in this balance that fundamental transformation becomes possible.

The practice of self-compassion in relationships shows up in specific moments:

During Arguments: When your voice shakes while setting a boundary, remind yourself that speaking up is brave, even if your delivery isn't perfect.

When old triggers surface, acknowledge them: "I'm feeling young and scared right now. That makes sense, given my history."

In Daily Interactions: When you catch yourself people-pleasing or hiding your true feelings—instead of shame, try curiosity. What need is this pattern trying to meet? What younger part of you is trying to stay safe?

In Quiet Moments: When you lie awake replaying conversations or imagining future scenarios, self—compassion matters most. Your mind tries to protect you, even if its methods are outdated.

The path of growth isn't about eliminating these moments. It's about meeting them differently. Instead of seeing triggers and patterns as personal failures, view them as opportunities for deeper understanding. You rewire old patterns each time you respond to yourself with kindness instead of criticism.

On those days when self-compassion feels impossible, when it feels too far and just too out of reach, when the voice of your inner critic is too loud? Start small. Take your hand and place it against the steady rhythm of your heart. Breathe gently, deeply, and intentionally, and then whisper to yourself, "This too belongs." because it does; all of it—the mess, the growth, the stumbling, the trying again, it's all part of becoming.

Journaling for Better Clarity

Recording one's thoughts can be therapeutic. It's almost like you're finally exhaling after holding your breath for too long. There's something about seeing your thoughts displayed on a blank page that makes them seem less overwhelming, less tangled. There's no pressure to show up perfectly. The thoughts come as they come, and your purpose in showing up on the page is to create a space where you can be completely honest with yourself: no filters, no need to explain or justify, and no fear of judgment—just you, your thoughts, and the gentle scratch of pen on paper. Sometimes, just naming a feeling is enough to loosen its grip on us.

This practice invites you to stop in a world that's always rushing, urging you to move, think, and respond more rapidly. To sit with your thoughts, let them breathe, and have a conversation with yourself—one where you're finally listening. In that listening, we often discover the clarity we've been searching for all along.

So, this is what you need to do: sit with the following questions. Please don't rush to answer them. Let them sink in. Maybe read them first thing in the morning when your mind is quiet or late at night when the world has slowed down. Take one at a time:

For Understanding Patterns:

- What do you do when you experience emotional vulnerability in your relationship?

- Which behaviors from your past relationships are you carrying into your current one?

- In what moments with your partner do you feel most authentically you?

- What's your earliest memory of feeling hurt in a relationship?

- How do you typically react when your partner needs space?

For Exploring Current Feelings:

- What are you most afraid to tell your partner right now?

- What recent moment fostered a strong connection with your partner?

- What do you need more of in your relationship right now?

- What triggers your anxiety in relationships?

- What characteristics in a person create a sense of safety for you?

For Growth and Self-Discovery:

- What parts of yourself do you hide from others? Why?
- How has your definition of love changed over the years?
- What's the hardest lesson your past relationships taught you?
- What do you wish others understood about your attachment style?
- How do you show love differently than how you receive it?

For Future Reflection:

- What kind of partner do you want to become?
- What boundaries do you need to set or maintain?
- What old relationship wounds still need healing?
- What patterns are you ready to break?
- How has your capacity for intimacy evolved?

Take your time with these questions. Some might find it simple to answer, and others might provoke unexpected emotions. Write honestly, write messily, write for yourself, and allow your answers to surprise you.

Set Realistic Personal Goals for Relational Improvement

Change doesn't happen overnight or in a vacuum. It would help if you had the right conditions, consistent care, and, most importantly, patience. Sometimes, we get so caught up in the big picture—wanting to be a better partner, hoping to fix all our relationship issues at once—that we forget change happens in small steps, one day at a time.

Vague goals like "communicate better" or "be more present" are about as helpful as saying "get fit" without a plan. Instead, I've found power in being specific and realistic. It's the difference between saying, "I want to be a better listener," and "I'm going to put my phone away during dinner conversations." One is a wish; the other is a plan.

Here's what works: Pick one small thing you can start today. Maybe it's taking three deep breaths before responding when you're upset. Perhaps it's sending one thoughtful text to your partner each morning. These aren't dramatic gestures, but they're doable. And doable goals, achieved consistently, create lasting change.

Having someone to share this journey with makes a world of difference. Not necessarily your partner (though they can be part of it), but someone who can check in on your progress, celebrate your small wins, and help you get back on track when you slip. Because you will slip—we all do. The key is getting back up and trying again.

Think of it this way: If you were learning to play an instrument, you wouldn't expect to master it in a week. You'd practice small pieces, celebrate when you get them right, and gradually build up to more complex pieces. Personal growth works the same way. Start small, be consistent, and trust that these tiny changes will add up to something beautiful.

Making Things Better: A Goal-Setting Exercise

Here's a way to make all of this more practical and digestible: Find a quiet moment, grab your journal, and let's map out what real, achievable change looks like for you:

Step 1: The Big Picture: Write down one area of your relationship you want to work on. Not everything—just one thing. Maybe it's how you handle conflicts, how you express affection, or how you maintain boundaries.

Step 2: Get Specific: Now break this down into observable behaviors. Instead of "handle conflict better," what would that look like?

- How would you speak differently?
- What would you do with your body?
- What specific actions would change?

Step 3: Create Your Ladder: Think of change as a ladder. You don't jump to the top—you climb one rung at a time.

- **Bottom rung:** What's the smallest possible step you could take tomorrow?
- **Middle rungs:** What gradual steps would build on this?
- **Top rung:** What's your ultimate vision?

For example, the bottom rung says, "I will pause for one breath before responding when upset." Middle rung: "I will express one feeling during conflicts without blaming." Top rung: "I will navigate disagreements while staying connected."

Step 4: Make It Measurable: For each rung on your ladder, add:

- When will you practice this? (Specific situations or times)
- How will you know you've done it? (Observable evidence)
- What might get in the way? (Potential obstacles)
- How will you support yourself? (Resources and self-care)

Step 5: Track Your Climb: Create a simple way to monitor your progress:

- What small wins will you celebrate?
- How will you remind yourself of your goals?
- Who can support you in this journey?
- How will you handle setbacks?

Don't focus on how perfect you can be; focus on the progress. Each small step counts as a significant contribution to personal growth. Each attempt matters. Each time you try again after a setback, you build new habits and neural pathways.

Keep this exercise somewhere visible. Review it weekly, adjust as needed, and celebrate every small victory.

Explore Past Relationship Patterns and Lessons Learned

Heartbreaks are awful. That deep, visceral ache that starts in your chest and somehow manages to seep into every corner of your existence. The way even mundane things; a song on the radio, a coffee shop you used to visit together, the way the light hits the sidewalk on a Sunday morning—become landmines of memory.

In all its awful glory, though, it is also one of our greatest teachers. Not right away, of course. First comes the pain, the anger, the what-ifs that keep you up at night, but eventually, if we're brave enough to look, each heartbreak leaves behind a map—a map of our patterns, triggers, most profound needs, and fears.

It would be amazing to avoid heartbreak altogether, but learning to read these maps and understanding that each relationship, even the ones that ended in flames, has something to teach us about ourselves is how we can learn to love better next time.

So, this is what we're going to do. Find a quiet space where you won't be interrupted. Get something to write with, and maybe a warm drink. We will map out your relationship patterns, but not in the clinical, detached way that makes you want to run for the hills. Instead, we will do this gently, with curiosity and compassion.

Start with your last three significant relationships. Write down their initials only—this isn't about them as people but the patterns they help us see. For each one, answer these questions:

The Beginning:

- What drew you to them?
- What was the first month like?
- What promises did you make to yourself?

The Middle:

- When did you first notice something felt off?
- What arguments kept repeating?
- How did you handle conflict?
- What aspects of yourself did you conceal?

The End:

- What was the final straw?
- What did you tell yourself to make it easier?
- What did you learn but maybe later forgot?

Now, look at your answers. Circle anything that shows up more than once. These are your patterns. Maybe you always fall for people who need fixing. Perhaps you consistently hide your needs until they explode. Maybe you keep choosing partners who remind you of someone from your past.

This isn't about judgment. It's about recognition. Saying, "Oh, there you are," to these patterns running the show behind the scenes.

Take a deep breath. Read what you've written one more time. Then ask yourself:

- Which patterns serve you?
- Which ones protect you from old hurts?
- Which ones are you ready to let go of?

Keep these answers somewhere safe. They're not just notes about your past, but clues about your future. A map showing where you've been and maybe, just maybe, where you'd like to go next.

Growth asks you to stand in the tension between who you've been and who you're becoming. Some days, this feels like shedding old skin. Other days, like trying to speak a new language, you're still learning. Our patterns, habits, and well-worn ways of moving through relationships made sense at one time. They served a purpose that is likely no longer needed. They kept you safe, helped you survive, and taught you to love with whatever tools you had.

Kristin Neff, Ph.D., is a prominent researcher, author, and professor best known for her pioneering work on self-compassion. She is an Associate Professor of Educational Psychology at the University of Texas at Austin and was among the first to define and empirically measure self-compassion. Her important research looks at how being kind to yourself can help your mental health and emotional strength.

Compassion is a cornerstone of positive psychology and plays a vital role in fostering healthy relationships, particularly when dealing with overthinking and communication struggles. At its core, compassion involves the awareness of someone's suffering, paired with the genuine desire to ease it. This study highlights three flows of compassion—toward others, from others, and self-compassion—and shows how they interact to create a supportive and emotionally connected environment. For relationships, this underscores the importance of both offering and receiving compassion, as well as cultivating self-compassion, to foster understanding and trust in communication.

Self-compassion, as defined by Dr. Neff, involves acknowledging your own imperfections with kindness, avoiding harsh self-judgment, and recognizing that everyone shares in the human experience of struggle. Overthinking in relationships frequently arises from internalized fears and anxieties, such as the fear of saying the wrong thing or being misunderstood. This concept is vital to grasp. Practicing self-compassion allows individuals to navigate these fears more constructively, creating space for open, non-defensive communication. Importantly, self-compassion isn't about avoiding emotions but about sitting with them and responding to yourself as you would to a friend in distress.

Neff developed the **Self-Compassion Scale**, a widely used tool for assessing self-compassion, and has published extensively in positive psychology. Her work emphasizes the importance of self-compassion as a healthier alternative to self-esteem, showing how it promotes emotional well-being, reduces anxiety, and fosters personal growth.

Graphic recorder Johnine Byrne created this wonderful graphic recording of Kristin Neff's three steps for self-compassion.

Chapter Seven

Strategies for Long-Term Relationship Health

We are safe partners when we're consistent, when our actions match our words, when we openly communicate our feelings, plans, and intentions, and when we own our mistakes. We can't build solid relationships with people who aren't willing and open to improving where necessary.

It's more than a "plan date nights and understand their love language" way. We mean it in the sense that we bear the grit of showing up, day after day, even when the shine has worn off. We opt to remain engaged when Netflix and quiet seem more appealing. We do the hard work of growing, not because some relationship guru told us to, but because we've decided that this person, this connection, is worth the effort.

Most of us know what a healthy relationship looks like from the outside, but living it is an entirely different story. It's messy. That's walking the fine line between holding on and letting go, between standing your ground and making space. It's learning to be uncomfortable together, to sit with the hard truths, to face the parts of ourselves we'd rather ignore because maybe that's what real relationship health is—not the absence of problems, but the courage to face them together.

Relationship health reveals itself in the ordinary moments. It lives in how you handle the everyday rhythms of shared life. It shows how you respond to your partner's changing moods and bridge the gap when one needs space and the other needs connection. It manifests in the hundred small choices you make each day—to turn toward each other, listen deeply, and reach out with understanding.

These daily moments create the foundation of lasting love. They become the quiet victories of choosing patience over frustration, understanding over judgment, and growth over comfort. They live in the courage to say "I'm here" when things get complicated, in the willingness to stay present through uncertainty.

Long-term relationship health grows in the soil of consistent care and in showing up fully. It flourishes where both partners can bring their whole selves, where growth, struggle, and success have a place. A relationship strong enough to hold all seasons of love.

Prioritize Shared Values and Visions for the Future

One of the challenging conversations Val and her partner had a few months into their relationship was about their family support systems. So they talked about kids and the future, and she mentioned how important it was for her to have her parents involved in their children's lives. His vision included Sunday dinners with extended family, grandparents attending school events, and passing down holiday traditions through generations.

When her partner shared their perspective, she learned his childhood painted a different picture. They grew up with families spread across the country, where independence was the norm and family gatherings happened once a year. The closeness Val envisioned felt foreign to their experience.

This conversation illuminated their core values, their understanding of family bonds, and expectations for the future. They explored these differences with openness and curiosity and learned that building a future together requires more than surface-level agreement. It demanded a deep understanding of each other's values and the willingness to create something unique to us. Their different backgrounds became the foundation for their traditions, the definition of family involvement, and their way forward.

Understanding Your Different Worlds

You and your partner are two completely different people, likely from different backgrounds, so it remains natural that you'll have different values, beliefs, and ways of seeing the world. These variations aren't something to fix or change—it's something to understand and work with.

Think about it: You grew up in your unique environment. Maybe one of you comes from a family where direct communication was the norm, while the other learned to read between the lines. Perhaps one of you was raised to believe career comes first, while the other grew up seeing family time as sacred. These aren't just preferences—they're deeply ingrained beliefs that shape how you move through life.

Core Values: Where You Meet and Where You Differ

Our values are the principles that guide our choices, shape our priorities, and influence how we move through life. They ultimately determine our most important decisions and reflect what matters most to us in our relationships and daily lives.

Family values manifest differently for each person. Some people thrive on weekly family gatherings and place importance on living near relatives. Others value creating solid boundaries and maintaining independent family units. Your views on family will influence significant life decisions, from choosing where to live to planning holiday celebrations.

Financial values often reveal our more profound beliefs about security and freedom. Some individuals find comfort in significant savings, while others prioritize experiences or property investments. Cultural traditions are also a contributing factor as well. The traditions we grew up with, the languages we speak, and the customs we follow shape our expectations for the future. Your perspective on career goals and leisure time will impact daily schedules, weekend activities, and long-term professional decisions.

When exploring values together, reflect on the principles that form the foundation of your life decisions, as these guide your actions and priorities. Consider where growth and adaptation can strengthen your bond, allowing you to navigate differences with understanding and flexibility. Think about how you can honor each other's fundamental beliefs, showing respect for the other's significant values. Finally, discuss the shared values you wish to develop as a couple, reiterating the importance of creating a unified vision for your future. This shared vision will inspire and motivate you to work towards a stronger, more aligned relationship.

Let me share what this looked like in Val's relationship. Her partner deeply valued financial security and saving for the future. They learned early on in their relationship that having a solid financial foundation provides peace of mind and opportunities. On the other hand, Val grew up believing experiences matter most—travel, concerts, and trying new restaurants.

Initially, this difference created tension in how they spent our money, but through open discussion, they realized both values could coexist. Creating a budget that prioritized saving while setting aside funds for experiences they shared helped them resolve what could have been a lifelong conflict into a win for their relationship. The goal is to understand the why behind each other's values and honor both. Now, planning for the future feels like something they do together rather than a source of conflict.

Building a Shared Vision

Building a shared vision starts with understanding that each person brings their dreams and aspirations to the relationship. One partner might envision running an international business empire with regular flights to Tokyo and Berlin. The other might dream of a small bookshop café filled with plants and the smell of fresh coffee, where people find both solitude and connection. These dreams might seem to occupy different universes, but looking deeper reveals the core elements that light up each person.

For the ambitious entrepreneur, someone who is driven, innovative, and constantly seeking growth, the journey often involves creating global connections that open doors to new opportunities and collaborations. It's about building something substantial, crafting a business that stands the test of time and delivers meaningful value. At its core, entrepreneurship is driven by the desire to make an impact, using business as a force for positive change and innovation in the world.

For the community builder, the focus lies in fostering local relationships, strengthening the bonds that bring people together, and creating a sense of belonging. They achieve this by creating peaceful spaces where individuals can connect, thrive, and feel at ease. By combining creativity with practicality, community builders bring innovative solutions to life, ensuring their efforts are both imaginative and sustainable.

Real possibilities emerge when you identify the common threads in their visions. Both of you might find you want to build something meaningful that connects people. This understanding opens doors to unexpected opportunities—perhaps a network of cultural spaces that combine local charm with global reach, where each location reflects its community while maintaining international connections.

Questions that help uncover shared vision:

    1. What energizes you most about your dream?

2. Which aspects of your vision appear most dynamic?

3. Where do individual dreams naturally intersect?

4. How can partners amplify each other's strengths?

Maintain Individual Identities While Nurturing the Relationship

You had a life and an identity before the relationship, so it doesn't mean that you don't deserve to have one. Your interests, passions, friendships, and goals remain essential to your identity. A healthy relationship creates space for both of you to continue growing as individuals while building something together.

Think about it this way: the qualities that attracted you to each other in the first place *probably* came from pursuing your paths, developing your interests, and cultivating your strengths. When you each maintain your spark, the relationship is dynamic and engaging.

Strong relationships thrive on the energy of two whole people choosing to share their lives, not two halves desperately trying to become whole. A strong relationship allows for pursuing personal goals, maintaining separate friendships, and sometimes simply enjoying solitude. This security in individual identities brings more to the relationship, not less.

Creating Space for Individual Growth

Your interests light you up in unique ways. Perhaps photography sparks your imagination, or rock climbing invigorates you. These passions deserve space to flourish. Each person brings their color to the relationship canvas—one partner might thrive in the quiet focus of writing, while the other comes alive through the adrenaline of competitive sports. These individual pursuits create a healthy ecosystem in your relationship. When one partner returns from a photography expedition, they bring back images, new perspectives, stories, and a refreshed spirit. When the other comes home from a climbing trip, they carry the confidence and accomplishment of reaching new heights. This energy flows into every aspect of the relationship.

Growing individually also means maintaining separate social circles. Your climbing group, book club, or weekly coffee dates with friends provide experiences and connections unique to you. These relationships offer different kinds of support and understanding than your romantic partnership can provide.

Think about your closest friendship; you might talk every day or once a month, but the connection remains strong because you both have full lives outside of each other. Romantic relationships work the same way. Time apart to pursue personal interests creates more engaging conversations and deeper appreciation when coming back together.

This space for individual growth reveals itself in small yet meaningful ways. It might involve reading different books and sharing the insights you gain, broadening each other's perspectives. It could mean taking separate classes and teaching each other new skills, fostering mutual learning and curiosity. Pursuing different career paths while wholeheartedly supporting each other's choices strengthens the bond of encouragement. Even maintaining separate hobbies while showing interest in your partner's passions creates a balance between individuality and connection, enriching the relationship through inspiring personal exploration.

When both partners are encouraged to grow individually, they bring their whole selves to the relationship. Creating a dynamic where both people choose to be together not out of need but out of a genuine desire to share their full, rich lives is the work.

The Power of Personal Time

Setting aside time for individual pursuits keeps both partners growing. Consider these ideas.

- A morning yoga practice.
- Weekly dinner with friends.
- Taking a class in something that interests you.
- Pursuing a personal project or goal.
- Spending quiet time alone to recharge.

Personal time allows each partner to maintain their sense of self while bringing fresh energy and perspectives. When both individuals experience personal satisfaction, their shared bond grows stronger.

Supporting Individual Dreams

Supporting your partner's individual growth strengthens your bond. This support appears in active, tangible ways:

When they share their dreams, listen with genuine curiosity, showing a sincere interest in their aspirations. Ask thoughtful questions that encourage them to explore their ideas more deeply, offering encouragement when doubts creep in. Show your care by remembering the details they share, demonstrating that their dreams matter to you. As they take action toward their goals, support them by creating space for focus and stepping in to handle extra responsibilities when needed. Help them connect with resources or people who can assist in their journey. And remember, celebrating even the small steps forward is crucial, as it acknowledges their progress and inspires them to keep going.

Yes, sometimes, supporting their dreams will mean taking a step back. Your partner might need uninterrupted time to write their novel, long hours to launch their business, weekends for their art exhibition, or early mornings for training. This time apart strengthens rather than threatens your connection. The way you respond to their achievements matters deeply. Each promotion, completed project, or personal milestone deserves real recognition, not just a quick "congratulations," but genuine excitement for their growth.

Making It Work

Nothing works if you don't put in the consistent effort to make it happen. Good intentions about maintaining individuality mean little without actual practices in place.

Start by blocking out non-negotiable time for your individual pursuits: those Tuesday evening art classes, your Saturday morning runs, that monthly weekend with friends, or that hour of solitude you need after work.

Then, create intentional moments to reconnect: Morning coffee together before the day begins, weekly date nights where phones stay put away, regular conversations about your individual journeys, or those shared celebrations of personal victories, big and small.

The key lies in being clear about your needs. "I need two hours on Thursday evening for my writing" works better than "I might want some time alone this week." Specific requests create clear agreements.

Habits That Strengthen Intimacy and Closeness

As a partner, understand that it is not your responsibility to take away all of your partner's insecurities. That kind of expectation leads to codependency and emotional exhaustion. Instead, building intimacy arises from crafting a place where both individuals sense security enough to be transparent, disclose their fears, and convey their needs.

True intimacy grows in the small moments of consistently showing up for each other. It's in the way you listen without trying to fix everything. It's in how you remember the little details they share. It's in the daily choice to stay present, even when it would be easier to retreat into your phone or lose yourself in distractions.

This kind of closeness doesn't happen by accident. It requires intention, awareness, and, most importantly, the understanding that intimacy isn't about perfect moments or grand gestures. It's about building trust through consistent, everyday actions that say, "I see you, I hear you, and I choose to understand you."

Holding Your Partner Closely

A kind partner is a present partner who pays attention to the small moments that make up a shared life. Kindness shows up in remembering how they like their coffee, sending that text when they have a big meeting, and making space for them on hard days with quiet understanding.

These daily acts of care build something sustainable. The foundation grows through meaningful conversations, where you listen to understand and learn. A weekly check-in over Sunday breakfast or a walk after dinner with full attention on each other creates a space where both people can easily share what's on their minds.

Building intimacy also means sharing experiences that light you both up, like looking at a new recipe together, planning that weekend trip, or sitting in comfortable silence while reading your books. These shared experiences create a tapestry of connection that grows richer each day.

Physical closeness matters in beautiful, simple ways. It lives in the brief touch as you pass each other in the hallway, the lingering hug after a long day, and the natural way you gravitate toward each other when sitting on the couch. This physical connection reminds each of you that you're seen, valued, and chosen.

Learning and Adaptability in the Relationship

Growth is a funny thing. When you think you've figured out your partner's morning routine, they wake up at 5 a.m. to meditate. When you've mastered their love language, they discover a new way they like to receive care. The relationship manual you thought you'd finally decoded needs a new chapter.

Because people grow, they evolve. The partner who once loved crowded parties might start craving quiet evenings at home. The one who needs constant conversation might learn to appreciate comfortable silence. The dedicated city dweller might suddenly dream of a garden.

This constant evolution makes relationships interesting. Each change, each new interest, and each shift in perspective offers a chance to learn each other all over again. It keeps the story fresh, adds new layers to your connection, and presents endless opportunities to grow individually and together.

Embracing Change Together

Change in relationships shows up in both big and small ways. Sometimes, it's a career shift that requires rethinking your daily routines. Other times, it's simpler, like adjusting to your partner's new passion for cooking, which has transformed your kitchen into a culinary experiment zone. A new job might mean different sleep schedules, adjusted meal times, or a shift in who handles morning responsibilities. A new hobby might transform your living space, change your spending weekends, or introduce you to new social circles.

Learning to flow with these changes strengthens your relationship. When your partner picks up a new hobby, get curious about it. Ask questions. Show interest. You don't need to share every passion, but understanding what excites them helps you stay connected as you grow.

This curiosity and support can look like:

- Making space for their new interests, both physically and emotionally.

- Asking specific questions about what they're learning or experiencing.

- Celebrating their small victories and breakthroughs.

- Adapting your shared routines to accommodate their growth.

- Showing appreciation for how their changes bring new energy to your relationship.

Supporting change means actively creating an environment where both partners have the confidence to explore, grow, and sometimes even fail. Their new business venture could fail, or the hobby might become less attractive after three months. Your role stays constant: being their safe harbor as they navigate these changes.

Making Growth a Shared Adventure

Growth naturally occurs when you explore new things together, whether taking a class neither of you has tried before, planning a trip to an unfamiliar destination, or learning to navigate challenges as a team. Creating new traditions that reflect who you are becoming as a couple further deepens your connection. These shared experiences not only build trust and understanding but also foster a deep sense of unity, offering a secure common ground while still honoring the unique journeys you are on.

The Art of Honest Conversations

Regular check-ins help you stay aligned as you grow. Unlike a performance review or interrogation, these conversations thrive when they come across as genuine. Look for moments when you both are at ease and ready to connect—maybe over weekend coffee, during evening walks, or while preparing dinner together.

Sharing current experiences can provide valuable insights into each other's lives and priorities. Reflect on which aspects of your routine energize you and identify areas needing more attention. Consider how supported you feel in pursuing your current goals, and explore what minor adjustments could help daily life flow more smoothly. These discussions foster connection and create opportunities for mutual growth and understanding.

Embracing changing needs allows you to adapt to each other's developing priorities and preferences, fostering a sense of reassurance and confidence. Reflect on whether your stress relievers have shifted recently and discuss what kind of support feels most helpful in the present moment. Consider which parts of your schedule benefit from added flexibility and how your ideal way of receiving care has grown. These conversations create space for growth and ensure your relationship remains attuned to one another's needs.

Expressing appreciation is a powerful tool that strengthens your connection by recognizing the value your partner brings to your life. Highlight specific ways they've supported you and share how their encouragement has contributed to your growth. Acknowledge the small, often overlooked gestures that make a meaningful difference in your day-to-day life. Let them know when their adaptability has been incredibly impactful, showing them that their efforts and flexibility are genuinely valued.

Looking forward together fosters a sense of partnership and instills hope for the future, making you feel optimistic and excited. Share your evolving dreams openly, without the pressure to figure out every detail, and discuss what excites or concerns you about what lies ahead. Keep each other updated on shifting priorities as your goals and circumstances change. Take time to explore new possibilities that pique your interests, creating a shared vision reflecting your growth as a team.

Keep these conversations balanced. They work best when both partners share and listen in equal measure. The goal isn't to solve everything in one talk but to maintain an ongoing dialogue that evolves with your relationship. Choose from the list of topics together. Both partners might not be in the same place with sharing, so it's okay to start small and build.

Staying Flexible in Roles and Responsibilities

Life demands flexibility. One partner might need to spend more time on household tasks in some weeks while the other focuses on a big project. Other times, you might need to reimagine how you share responsibilities completely.

The key is understanding that roles can shift. What worked last year might need adjustment now. Those carefully divided chore lists and routines you created? Think of them as rough guidelines rather than rigid rules.

Stay open to rearranging responsibilities based on the following:

Changing Seasons of Life

- One partner starting a new job or degree.

- Health challenges that require extra support.

- Family obligations that demand more attention.

- Busy periods at work that drain energy.

Personal Growth and Evolution

- New interests that take up more time.

- Shifting career priorities.
- Changes in how you each recharge.
- Different stress management needs.

Daily Energy Flows

Morning person vs. night owl tendencies.

High-energy days vs. recovery days.

Creative periods that need protection.

Times when the focus comes naturally.

This flexibility might look like:

- Trading morning routine duties when sleep patterns change.
- Shifting cooking responsibilities during busy work periods.
- Adjusting weekend activities to allow for new pursuits.
- Taking turns being the primary support person.

The goal isn't perfect balance every day. Instead, aim for overall fairness over time, understanding that some weeks one person carries more while others reverse. What matters is maintaining open communication about capacity and needs and being willing to step up when your partner needs extra support.

Chapter Eight

Cultural Sensitivity and Embracing Differences

In Nigeria, it is common and expected that you will live with your husband's parents even after marriage. The eldest son often cares for aging parents; his wife joins this family structure. Through our Western lens, this seems unimaginable, but for Nigerians, a deep sense of family obligation, community, and intergenerational support in their culture is essential. Can you understand how my cultural assumptions shaped my initial reaction?

Our views on relationships, family, and love are influenced by the cultures we grow up in. What seems "normal" or "right" to one person might feel foreign to another. These differences show up in small ways—how we express affection, handle conflict, celebrate milestones, and, more significantly, how we view family structures, gender roles, or financial responsibilities.

The beauty of cross-cultural relationships lies not in erasing these differences, but in learning to navigate them with curiosity and respect. Each cultural perspective offers its wisdom about love, commitment, and connection. When we open ourselves to understanding different viewpoints, we enrich our understanding of relationships.

Understanding Cultural Context

Think about something as simple as saying, "I love you." In some cultures, these words flow freely and often. In others, love is shown through actions rather than words. One partner might expect verbal affirmation daily, while the other demonstrates love through acts of service, following their cultural norms. Intercultural marriages involve spouses from different racial or ethnic backgrounds. In the United States, the prevalence of such marriages has been increasing over the years. According to a 2017 report by the Pew Research Center, 17% of all U.S. newlyweds in 2015 had a spouse of a different race or ethnicity, marking a significant rise from 3% in 1967.

More recent data from 2019 indicates that this figure has continued to grow, with 19% of newlyweds marrying someone of a different race or ethnicity. These differences can extend into every aspect of your relationship.

Family Dynamics

- In many Asian cultures, living with parents after marriage isn't just expected—it expresses filial piety and respect.

- Some cultures view family as an intimate part of the relationship, involved in significant decisions.

- Others maintain strict boundaries between nuclear and extended families.

- The role of siblings, grandparents, and extended family varies dramatically across cultures.

Decision-Making

- Some cultures expect big decisions to be made by the eldest male family member.

- Others prioritize joint decision-making between partners.

- Some involve the entire extended family in significant choices.
- The balance of power between partners often reflects cultural expectations.

Financial Management

- Certain cultures keep finances strictly between spouses.
- Others view money as belonging to the extended family unit.
- Some have specific customs about who handles day-to-day expenses versus long-term savings.
- Cultural views on debt, saving, and sharing resources with family can vary widely.

Public Affection and Social Behavior

- What's considered romantic in one culture might be inappropriate in another.
- Some cultures have strict rules about physical contact in public.
- Others encourage open displays of affection.
- Even simple gestures like holding hands can carry different cultural meanings.

Celebrations and Milestones

- Marriage ceremonies and their significance vary enormously across cultures.
- Some cultures mark relationship stages with specific rituals, which may be religious or traditional ceremonies.

- Achievement and success in relationships are celebrated differently.

Recognizing these cultural differences is essential, as it helps partners develop empathy and understand why certain behaviors are perceived differently. One partner might feel suffocated by levels of family involvement that the other considers completely normal. Financial decisions that seem logical to one may appear perplexing to the other. Similarly, a lack of affection for one partner might be a profound expression of respect in the other's cultural context. Even celebrations that seem extravagant to one could hold deep and fundamental significance for the other. This underscores the importance of understanding and appreciating these diverse perspectives, fostering a sense of compassion and understanding in relationships.

The key isn't to dismiss these differences but to understand how they've shaped each partner's expectations and needs. When you understand the 'why' behind cultural practices, what initially seemed strange, often makes perfect sense.

Learning Through Listening

We've talked a fair bit about listening throughout the book. However, listening takes on even more significance when it comes to understanding cultural differences. Not just about hearing words, but understanding the entire context of your partner's cultural identity.

When your partner shares stories about their culture, they invite you into their world. They may recount festivals from their childhood or illuminating the profound significance of certain family traditions. These sharing moments are opportunities to understand what they do and why these practices matter.

Patience is a key value in cultural listening. It's about approaching conversations with openness and curiosity, and temporarily setting aside your cultural framework to understand the perspective of others. This practice requires resisting the urge to compare everything to your own experiences, as it can limit your understanding. Some concepts may need more direct translations, which require patience and deeper exploration. Emotional significance might not always be immediately apparent, so it's important to allow time to uncover its importance. Finally, it's about acknowledging that some traditions may initially seem unusual or even unsettling, but with understanding, they can reveal profound value and connection.

Try exploring these areas through conversation:

Family Dynamics and Traditions

- "What role did extended family play in your upbringing?"
- "Which family traditions bring back the strongest memories?"
- "How were important decisions made in your family?"
- "What values were emphasized in your household?"

Cultural Identity and Values

- "What aspects of your culture make you feel most proud?"
- "Which traditions do you find most meaningful?"
- "How has your culture shaped your view of relationships?"
- "What cultural practices help you feel connected to your roots?"

Future Hopes and Concerns

- "Which cultural traditions do you want to maintain in our relationship?"
- "What worries you about blending our different cultural back-

grounds?"

- "How can we honor both our cultural identities?"
- "What new traditions could we create together?"

Cultural sharing often happens in layers. What might seem like a simple story about a holiday celebration could reveal deeper values about family, community, and spirituality. Stay curious, ask thoughtful follow-up questions, and be patient as understanding develops.

Creating Space for Both Cultures

Building a relationship across cultures means crafting a unique bond that honors and integrates the richness of both traditions. In daily life, this can involve incorporating food traditions from both cultures, allowing meals to become a shared celebration of diversity. It includes celebrating holidays from each background and fostering a deeper appreciation for each other's heritage. Honoring family expectations helps maintain respect and harmony in relationships. Together, you can create new traditions that blend elements of both cultures, symbolizing your shared journey and the inspiring process of mutual growth.

Building a cross-cultural relationship involves thoughtful effort and mutual understanding. Learning key phrases in each other's languages bridges gaps and shows a willingness to embrace each other's heritage. Understanding and adapting to different communication styles fosters clarity and reduces misunderstandings. Respecting cultural approaches to conflict resolution, with a strong emphasis on empathy, promotes harmony, even when methods differ. Finding a middle ground in expressing emotions helps balance diverse ways of connecting and creating a shared language of understanding and support.

Practical Ways to Learn and Share

The cultural exchange begins in your own home. Perhaps it's the kitchen, where your partner's favorite dish mingles with morning coffee, or the living room, where a film from their homeland plays. These moments matter more than planned cultural excursions or formal celebrations. Ask your partner to teach you their mother's recipe—not just the ingredients, but the stories behind each step. Learn why certain spices remind them of home or how their grandmother could tell when a dish was perfect without ever measuring.

When your partner shares their language, listen for more than just words. Learn which phrases carry weight beyond their literal translation. To know why certain expressions make them laugh or why some topics require careful phrasing offers glimpses into their cultural worldview.

Music opens another door. Create playlists that blend both your cultural soundtracks. Let them explain why certain songs matter, what memories they hold, and which ones are played at every family gathering. Share the artists who shaped your cultural understanding.

Engage with their community. Observe how relationships work, how respect is shown, and how celebrations unfold. Notice the unspoken rules—who speaks first at gatherings, how elders are treated, what makes people comfortable or uncomfortable. These subtle dynamics reveal more than any cultural handbook could.

Your shared space becomes a living museum of both backgrounds—photographs that tell family stories, objects that carry meaning, and traditions that you choose to maintain or adapt. Create room for both cultures to breathe and evolve together.

Spotting Cultural Friction Points

Cultural misunderstandings often surface in subtle ways before becoming apparent conflicts. Your partner might become quiet when you handle a situation in a way that sits uncomfortably with them. You might feel uncomfortable with how they interact with their family without understanding why. These deserve attention before they grow into more significant issues.

Watch for the small tensions that emerge in daily life. Consider the possibility that your partner hesitates when you make decisions without consulting family or feels uncomfortable when you address their parents by first name. These aren't just personal preferences—they often reflect deeper cultural values about respect, family hierarchy, and relationship boundaries.

Family dynamics reveal these cultural gaps most clearly. What one partner sees as everyday family involvement, the other might experience as intrusive. The partner who grew up with weekly family dinners might struggle to understand their partner's need for more independence. In the same way, one person's casual approach to dropping by family members' homes might clash with another's formal visiting customs.

Even simple daily routines can become friction points. Meal times, for instance, carry cultural weight, not just when to eat, but how to eat, what to eat, and who should be present. Morning and evening rituals, weekend social expectations, and holiday celebrations all follow cultural patterns we might not even realize we're carrying.

The way we express care and affection often reveals cultural differences, too. Public displays of affection, gift-giving customs, and methods of showing respect can vary dramatically across cultures. One partner might show love through physical affection, while the other demonstrates care through practical support, each following their cultural norms.

Pay attention when you notice repeated sighs, unusual quietness, or defensive responses to certain situations. These reactions often signal underlying cultural friction that needs addressing. The key isn't to judge these differences but to approach them with curiosity and respect, seeing them as opportunities to deepen your understanding of each other's cultural frameworks.

Moving Beyond "That's Just How We Do It"

Culture sits bone-deep. It's in how we celebrate, how we mourn, how we show love, how we express anger. When someone questions these ingrained ways of being, it can feel like they're questioning who we are at our core. It's no surprise that cultural differences in relationships can appear very personal and challenging to navigate.

Instead of defending your cultural practices or dismissing your partner's, approach these moments with a generous amount of curiosity. Think about how your partner's culture has shaped their understanding of love, respect, and relationships, just as yours has shaped you. Their approach to family dynamics, conflict resolution, or celebration carries generations of wisdom and meaning.

The path forward involves asking questions that invite deeper sharing: "Help me understand why this matters to you." "What values does this tradition protect?" "What would feel disrespectful about doing it differently?"

These conversations work best when you:

- Listen without planning your defense.
- Acknowledge that both approaches might hold value.
- Look for wisdom in unfamiliar practices.

Consider the couple who clashed over handling family involvement in their decisions. Rather than arguing about whose family system was "right," they explored why each approach developed. They discovered that one partner's culture emphasized collective wisdom and family harmony, while the others valued individual growth and autonomy. Understanding these underlying values helped them create an approach that honored both perspectives.

The goal is to reach a point where you both understand why these practices matter so deeply to each person. This understanding creates space for both partners to feel respected while building something new together.

Finding Middle Ground

Direct versus indirect. Individual versus collective. Fast versus slow. Cultural clashes often sound simple on the surface but cut straight to our core beliefs about how life should work. Like the couple who spent three years negotiating Sunday dinners, his family expected weekly attendance, while her family valued spontaneous, pressure-free gatherings or the partners who discovered their different ways of handling money weren't just personal preferences but reflected generations of their families' relationships with financial security.

When my friend described managing her intercultural relationship, she said it felt like learning to write with her non-dominant hand, awkward at first, but eventually leading to new skills and perspectives she'd never considered before. Success lies in reimagining possibilities. Take the couple who blended their approaches to elder care: they created a guest house where parents could stay for extended visits, honoring both filial piety and independence. Another pair merged their contrasting conflict styles by starting difficult conversations through letters, then moving to face-to-face discussions, combining one partner's need for direct communication with the other's preference for thoughtful processing.

Real solutions emerge when we stop trying to pick the "right" culture and start building bridges between them. It's about creating something new that carries the essence of both worlds while being uniquely yours.

Building Your Own Cultural Bridge

Think of a Thanksgiving table where dumplings sit next to turkey or a wedding where salsa music flows into Bollywood beats. These moments represent more than just mixing traditions—they showcase the art of creating something entirely new from the richness of two cultural worlds.

Building cultural bridges starts in daily life. One couple transformed their morning routine into a blend of Vietnamese coffee rituals and American breakfast customs. Another family created their own unique holiday by combining Diwali's light and sweets with Christmas trees and carols. These weren't compromises but creative celebrations of both heritages.

Weekend gatherings might feature your grandmother's secret recipe alongside your partner's family's traditional dishes. Family celebrations can weave together different languages, mixing familiar phrases with new expressions until they become your unique dialect. Even how you decorate your home can tell the story of both backgrounds, with art pieces from one culture complementing traditional crafts from another.

The beauty lies in evolution. Each year, each celebration, each shared moment, adds another layer to your unique cultural tapestry. Your children might grow up knowing both one grandmother's prayers and another's folk tales. They'll inherit not just two cultures but the gift of seeing how love can bridge any cultural gap.

This fusion becomes your family's signature, something uniquely yours that still honors its roots. It's about creating traditions that make both partners feel seen, valued, and celebrated.

When Things Get Stuck

Cultural clashes can hit hard, stirring up emotions that run generations deep. That argument about how to raise your children might not be about bedtimes or discipline. It might be about honoring ancestors, preserving identity, and passing down values that have sustained your family through hardships.

In these moments, allow yourself to pause and let the emotions exist without rushing to smooth them over your partner's fierce reaction to how you handle money, which might stem from their grandparents' stories of survival. Your strong feelings about family obligations might carry the weight of centuries of tradition.

Give these big feelings room to breathe. Cultural understanding rarely happens in a single conversation. Sometimes, it takes weeks of gentle questions, months of observing family dynamics, and years of participating in traditions before the deeper meanings emerge. Watch how your partner's family handles similar situations. Notice what makes their eyes light up when they talk about home.

A healthy relationship is one where both of you feel safe enough to navigate these differences, so you both listen and listen without defense when your partner explains why your well-intended actions felt disrespectful. It means holding space for them to miss their culture's way of doing things without feeling guilty. And remember that these don't always need solutions; sometimes, they need acknowledgment, respect, and the patience to let understanding grow naturally between you.

The Weight of Unspoken Expectations

Sometimes, Lili looks at her partner and reminds herself that this is his first time navigating certain situations in this life, and because of that, she needs to be kind to him. he couldn't possibly know that in her culture, leaving food on one's plate is seen as wasteful and disrespectful, or that certain questions about family matters might touch on topics considered private.

These unspoken rules run deep; they're the knowledge we absorb through years of family dinners, holiday celebrations, and quiet observations. They have become so natural to us that we forget that we should explain them, like how some of us were taught never to show up empty-handed to someone's home or how expressing disagreement with elders might be seen as a sign of disrespect in some cultures.

When these invisible guidelines meet different cultural expectations, misunderstandings naturally arise. Your partner might think they're being polite by refusing seconds at your family dinner, not realizing this could be interpreted as a rejection of hospitality. Or they might share family news openly, unaware that some issues are kept within strict family boundaries in your culture.

The beauty exists in that space where we learn to recognize these moments not as failures but as opportunities to understand each other better. Each misunderstanding, each confused look, and each bit of tension carries the potential for deeper connection only if we're willing to explain our cultural perspectives with patience and listen to our partner with genuine curiosity.

Starting These Conversations

Start with your cultural blind spots, those deeply ingrained practices and beliefs you carry without question. It might surface unexpectedly, like when your partner questions why you always call your aunties for advice before making big decisions or insist on specific ceremonies around birthdays.

All of this will be jarring at first. When someone asks about practices that feel as natural as breathing, it's easy to become defensive. But these questions offer precious opportunities to examine and share the cultural framework that shapes your world.

Think about the traditions that feel most automatic to you. Maybe it's how you automatically defer to elders in conversations or tend to remove your shoes before entering a home. Perhaps it's in how you celebrate achievements - some cultures mark every small win with elaborate gatherings, while others prefer quiet acknowledgment.

When sharing these cultural practices, frame them as your lived experience rather than universal law. Instead of saying, "You should always show respect by..." try "In my family, we show respect by..." This subtle shift invites conversation rather than compliance. It opens the door for your partner to share their cultural perspectives without feeling judged or corrected.

Remember that explaining your culture might require unpacking layers of meaning. What seems like a simple practice—serving elders first at meals—might carry deep cultural significance about respect, hierarchy, and family values. Take time to explore not just the what of your cultural practices but the why behind them. These conversations work best when approached with humility and curiosity. Share your cultural stories as gifts rather than guidelines, inviting your partner into a deeper understanding of your world while remaining open to learning about theirs.

Setting Clear Cultural Boundaries

Boundary work is healthy and is vital to making relationships work. Concerning our cultural boundaries, this work becomes even more delicate because we were required to handle generations of tradition, family expectations, and deeply held beliefs about how life should be lived.

These boundaries often emerge around fundamental aspects of life: Time with family—how frequently, how long, and in what ways you engage with extended family. Sacred practices—which traditions must be maintained and which can be adapted. Language and communication—how some topics should be discussed or whether they can be discussed in all personal space—what constitutes respect and disrespect in daily interactions.

Honesty and context matter in the grander. Scheme of these. Instead of simply stating, "I can't miss Sunday family dinner," share what this tradition means: "In my culture, Sunday dinners are where we maintain family bonds, where younger generations learn from elders, where we keep our cultural stories alive."

On that same note, when certain cultural practices make you uncomfortable, explain your discomfort through your cultural lens: "In my upbringing, openly discussing personal matters was seen as disrespecting privacy. While I'm learning to be more open, I need time to adjust to this different way of sharing." The goal isn't to create rigid lines but to help your partner understand the cultural weight behind your needs. This understanding can transform what might seem like inflexibility into an opportunity for deeper cultural appreciation.

A partner's enforcement of cultural boundaries is not their choice to reject you. Instead, they protect values that matter deeply to them, traditions that keep them connected to their roots, and practices that give their lives meaning. When we frame them this way, setting boundaries becomes an act of care—both for ourselves and the relationship.

When Values Clash

You and your partner exist as individuals first, shaped by different families, traditions, and cultural stories; each carries a unique set of values, beliefs, and ways of moving through the world that were ingrained long before you met.

Our cultural values are like the roots of two different trees. Some roots run parallel, nurturing similar beliefs about love, respect, or family. Others grow in opposite directions, pulling you toward different approaches to life's challenges. The strength of these roots—how deeply they reach, how firmly they hold—determines how much flexibility exists for finding common ground.

Understanding this helps explain why inevitable conflicts feel so immovable. When you clash over how to support aging parents or disagree about financial priorities, you're not just arguing about practical decisions. You're navigating between cultural imperatives that have sustained your families for generations.

Success often lies in identifying where your cultural roots can intertwine and where they need space to grow separately. Like the couples who find harmony by maintaining separate spiritual practices while creating shared rituals for significant life events. Or partners who blend different approaches to child-rearing by consciously choosing which aspects of each culture to pass on.

You don't have to uproot either set of values, but cultivate a shared space where you both can flourish; you develop new traditions that honor your backgrounds or find creative ways to meet cultural obligations while respecting individual needs.

Building Ongoing Understanding

Cultural understanding unfolds like a story that never quite reaches its last page. Each year brings new chapters—maybe it's watching your partner discover the meaning behind a tradition they once questioned or finding yourself moved by a celebration that used to feel foreign.

The most meaningful moments will often come unexpectedly, like when your mother teaches your partner her secret family recipe, speaking in broken English and gestures, yet somehow creating a bridge of understanding that transcends language. Or when your partner's grandmother shares stories of the old country, you suddenly understand why certain habits and beliefs run so deep.

This is ongoing, and you'll learn to see your culture through fresh eyes as you explain it to someone else. You discover new aspects of your partner's heritage that help define who they are and why they move through the world as they do.

You are both writing a new cultural story that honors where you both come from while celebrating where you're going; this is how traditions evolve, how cultures blend and grow, and how love creates something entirely new from the treasures of the past.

Chapter Nine

Healing and Wholeness—The Way Back to Yourself

We will inevitably change as we live, which means our relationships will also change. So, maybe there would be a little less suffering if we all chose to love with acceptance of our inevitable revolutions.

Nobody tells you that healing often looks like unlearning—unlearning the need to be perfect, the habit of making yourself small, and the idea that love means abandoning your boundaries. Sometimes, the bravest thing isn't changing who you are but finally having the courage to meet yourself exactly as you are.

Reclaiming Parts of Yourself Lost in Relationships

Overthinking tends to kill the most beautiful parts of us. The spontaneous parts. The wild parts. The parts that used to dance in the kitchen without checking if anyone was watching. The parts that would sing off-key without apologizing. The parts that would say what they meant without running it through a hundred filters first.

You can lose part of yourself and barely notice. A habit here, a preference there. Small compromises that don't feel like compromises at the time you make yourself easier to love—or so you think. Until one day, you can't remember the last time you'd laughed without wondering if you were being too loud.

This happens when we treat ourselves like a rough draft that needs constant editing. We erase our edges, smooth out our quirks, and delete the things that make us real. We become so good at being palatable that we forget how to be true.

The path back to yourself doesn't start with grand gestures. It begins with tiny acts of rebellion against your self-censorship. Wearing the bright shoes you love but tucked away because someone once called them "too much." Playing your favorite song on repeat because it feeds your soul, even if others don't get it. You are speaking your truth at that moment instead of finding the perfect words.

The truth is that the parts of you that feel "too much" —too sensitive, too intense, too different are essential pieces of your wholeness, and reclaiming them isn't just about personal healing. It's about showing up in your relationships as a complete, complex, beautifully imperfect human being.

Healing Codependent Patterns

Codependency is an ugly word. We toss it around in therapy sessions and self-help books like it's just another clinical term, but it's messier than that. It's the way you lose your breath when someone's mood shifts. It's how you've become fluent in reading micro-expressions because your safety once depended on predicting someone else's emotions. That voice in your head says love means never causing discomfort, never having needs, never being "too much."

Codependency is essentially an unhealthy relationship pattern where one person's sense of purpose and identity becomes excessively wrapped up in taking care of or controlling another person.

Codependency happens when:

1. Your self-worth and emotional wellbeing depend heavily on another person's approval, needs, or problems

2. You prioritize someone else's needs above your own to an extreme degree

3. You feel responsible for solving other people's problems or "rescuing" them

4. You struggle to set healthy boundaries or say "no"

5. You feel anxious or guilty when not actively helping the other person

A classic example is someone in a relationship with a person struggling with addiction. Codependents enable addiction while believing they're being supportive, organizing their lives around the addict, and finding purpose in being "needed".

Codependency affects not only romantic relationships but also those between parents and children, friends, or family members. The key distinction from healthy caring is that in codependency, there's an imbalance where one person's identity becomes defined by their caretaking role, often at the expense of their own wellbeing and independence. We learn these patterns early. Maybe you were the child who became an emotional caretaker for your parents. Perhaps you knew that love meant walking on eggshells or that your worth was measured by how useful you could be to others. These lessons didn't come with warning labels. They came wrapped in phrases like "being considerate" and "putting others first."

The tricky part about healing codependency is that society often rewards these behaviors. You're the friend everyone counts on, the partner who invariably understands, the one who can handle everything. Your ability to anticipate others' needs makes you "thoughtful." Your tendency to put yourself last makes you "selfless." But at what cost?

It shows up in relationships in subtle ways:

- Apologizing for having needs.

- Feeling responsible for other people's emotions.

- Making yourself smaller to make others comfortable.

- Losing your sense of self in relationships.

- Being drawn to people who need "fixing."

The healing starts with uncomfortable truths, like recognizing that what you thought was empathy might be hypervigilance. What you label as love might be closer to control, trying to manage others' feelings and behaviors so you can feel safe.

Breaking these patterns means learning new equations:

- Love ≠ Taking responsibility for others' emotions.

- Care ≠ Sacrificing your own needs.

- Support ≠ Losing yourself.

- Worth ≠ Usefulness to others.

This healing isn't linear. Some days, you'll catch yourself falling into old patterns—overextending, people-pleasing, boundary-crossing. The difference is that now you notice. Now you can pause and ask yourself: "Is this genuine care, or is this codependency? Am I showing up or trying to control the outcome?"

The real work lies in building a new relationship with yourself. It's learning that you don't have to earn the right to exist, that your needs aren't inconvenient, and that you can care deeply about others without becoming their emotional caretaker.

Building self-trust begins with small, intentional acts that affirm your confidence and boundaries. Practice saying no without explaining yourself, allowing your decisions to stand independently. Let others experience their emotions without rushing to fix or manage them, trusting their ability to process their feelings. Embrace moments of discomfort by resisting the urge to immediately smooth things over, showing courage in the face of challenging emotions. Finally, express your needs openly and without apology, reinforcing the value of your voice and prioritizing your well-being.

Remember that codependency developed as a survival mechanism; it kept you safe once. But now it's time to learn new ways of relating to yourself and others that allow for mutual care without self-abandonment, honor, connection, and independence.

The goal isn't to stop caring. It's to care without losing yourself in the process, to love without making yourself responsible for outcomes you can't control, and to show up fully while letting others do the same.

Mapping Your Patterns

Take some time with your journal, then draw a line down the middle of a page, creating two columns.

In the first column, write: "What did love look like in my home growing up?" Think about:

- Who was the emotional caretaker?

- How were feelings expressed (or not expressed)?

- What earned you praise?

- What behaviors were rewarded?

- What made you feel safe?

In the second column, write: "How do these patterns show up in my relationships now?" For example:

- If praise comes from caring for others, do you still seek worth through caretaking?

- If emotions were unsafe, would you still work to keep everyone happy?

- If attention came from achievement, do you still need to over-achieve to feel valued?

Now, on a new page, explore these questions:

- When do you feel most like yourself? (Notice if your answer involves being helpful to others)

- What would you do differently in your life if you knew no one would be upset with you? (Pay attention to how long it takes to answer this)

- What parts of yourself did you hide to keep relationships smooth? (Be specific - maybe it's your laugh, your opinions, your dreams)

- Think of the last time you said "yes" when you wanted to say "no."

- What were you afraid would happen if you said no?

- Where did you learn this fear?

- What do you need to feel safe saying no?

Write A Letter To Your Younger Self – Here is an example:

Dear Younger Me,

I see you, and I understand the challenges you faced. You were doing your best to survive in a world that often felt overwhelming and unpredictable. Your adaptability, your tendency to say yes when you wanted to say no, and your habit of smoothing over conflicts were all strategies to stay safe and feel loved. You were protecting yourself the best way you knew how, and I want you to know that your choices were not wrong. You did what you needed to do.

But I wish you had known, even back then, just how inherently worthy you are. Your value was never tied to how much you could give, how much you could fix, or how little space you could take up. You deserved love and respect simply because you existed, not because of what you could do for others. That truth hasn't changed. You don't need to earn the right to be seen, heard, and cared for.

Now, let's actively work together to unlearn patterns that no longer serve us. Let's unlearn the need to apologize for our needs, rush to fix everything, and make ourselves small for the comfort of others. Let's let go of the idea that conflict is something to fear or that saying no is selfish. These beliefs once helped us, but they're not helping us anymore.

Instead, let's create new patterns that feel truer to who we are now. Let's say no when we mean it and trust that it's enough. Let's allow others to feel their emotions without taking responsibility for them. Let's sit with discomfort and know it won't last forever. Most of all, let's express our needs unapologetically, trusting that we deserve to be cared for just as we are.

I'm here with you every step of the way, cheering you on and holding you close when things feel hard. Remember, healing doesn't mean erasing the past—it means writing a new story for the future, where we get to thrive, not just survive. And when old patterns resurface, as they sometimes will, come back to this letter. Let it remind you that you are your own best source of comfort and that you've always had what it takes to grow.

With love and compassion,

Your Older Self

Trusting Your Intuition

The body knows; it knows joy. It knows sadness, and it knows what anxiety, what grief, and what peace feels like. The mind gets in the way, questioning every gut feeling and analyzing every instinct until we can't tell the difference between intuition and fear.

Some people spend years dismissing their body's signals because they may have seen or they had been told they were highly irrelevant; that tightness in your chest during certain conversations? Maybe you were too, and you were just overly sensitive. Did you notice your shoulders would creep toward your ears around certain people? Just stress, maybe? The sudden exhaustion that would hit after forcing yourself to socialize when you just needed solitude? It's probably just poor sleep.

However, our bodies are much wiser than our minds try to rationalize. That gut feeling you get about a situation isn't just anxiety speaking—it's years of collected data and countless subtle observations your conscious mind hasn't even registered. It's your body's way of protecting you, guiding you, trying to tell you something important.

To learn to trust your gut, you must accustom yourself to turning back into that frequency your body's been broadcasting all along, to recognize that your instincts, even the uncomfortable ones, deserve your attention.

When you start listening, really listening, you might notice:

- How your breathing changes around certain people.

- The way your energy shifts in different environments.

- Which conversations leave you feeling lighter or heavier.

- When your shoulders finally relax.

These aren't random physical responses. They're your internal compass trying to guide you back to yourself. Back to what feels authentic, what feels right, what feels safe, not what your overthinking mind has decided should feel right.

You were born knowing how to do that. The trick is unlearning how you've been taught to doubt it, question your own knowledge, and override your body's wisdom with logic, rationale, and other people's expectations. What they rarely tell us—but I'm choosing to share with you because it's too valuable to keep hidden—is that intuition doesn't rely solely on a 'sixth sense.'; it's the accumulated wisdom of your lived experience speaking to you through your body's signals. It's your true self trying to be heard above the noise of overthinking.

Find your way back to trusting yourself and knowing that you don't need to solve every feeling, interpret every interaction, or anticipate every outcome. Return to the belief that you are enough, even when your mind tries to tell you otherwise.

Overcoming overthinking isn't about achieving perfect mental clarity or silencing every doubt. It's about taking control and embracing the present moment, even when uncertainty feels uncomfortable. It's about showing up fully in your relationships, even when your mind insists on first running through every possible scenario.

Your worth isn't measured by how well you can predict outcomes or solve every problem before it arises. You don't need to earn the right to take up space in someone's life—your existence is enough. Your feelings are valid, even when they defy logic, and it's okay to trust the quiet knowing, that gut feeling or intuition, that resides deep within you.

You can care deeply without taking on the weight of everything. Your presence, as it is, is enough, even when your overthinking mind tries to convince you otherwise. Remember, growth comes from perfect understanding and learning to let go, trust, and be.

Repeat this mantra: I trust my intuition more than my anxious thoughts. I release the need to control what others think of me. I choose presence over perfection. I am allowed to feel without analyzing every emotion. My worth exists independent of others' reactions. I trust the timing of my growth and healing. I permit myself to be human. My sensitivity is my strength. I am safe in uncertainty. Love doesn't require certainty.

May you find your way back to yourself, one present moment at a time.

Keeping the Connection Strong

Now that you've explored the tools and insights to quiet your overthinking and build better communication, it's time to share your experience with others who might need the same guidance.

By leaving your honest opinion of *The Overthinker's Guide to Relationship Communication* on Amazon, you're not just sharing your thoughts—you're helping others discover a resource that could change their relationships for the better.

Thank you for being part of this journey. This book's mission—to help people communicate with ease and connect with heart—lives on because of readers like you. This book is a tool and resource, but it does not replace the role of a therapist and if you feel you need to seek professional help, to please do so. My goal is to empower readers with resources for improved mental health. Click here to leave a review or scan the QR code below.

https://www.amazon.com/review/review-your-purchases/?asin=B0DNNQ5HG7

Quick Start Guide
Silence the Doubt and Flip the Script

That analyzing voice in your head isn't your enemy—it's your mind trying to protect you. But when overthinking holds you back from expressing yourself, it's time to channel those racing thoughts into meaningful dialogue.

Think of your thoughts as seeds of insight rather than sources of anxiety. Each worry that crosses your mind carries a valuable perspective that, when shared thoughtfully, can deepen your connections and lead to transformative conversations.

The secret isn't to silence your mind–it's to transform its energy into genuine curiosity about others' perspectives. You create space for honest, enriching exchanges when you approach conversations with authentic interest instead of predetermined assumptions. Your overthinking becomes a superpower for empathy and understanding rather than a barrier to connection.

By learning to voice your thoughts with intention, you're not just breaking free from the overthinking cycle–you're turning your inner monologue into bridges of understanding with others. The very concerns that keep you up at night could be the beginning of conversations that change your perspective and those around you.

Practices:

Nagging Thought: *They didn't text back. They must be upset with me.*

Reframe: "They might be busy. Not every delay means something is wrong. I can check in later, calmly."

How to Discuss: "Hey, I noticed I sometimes feel anxious when I don't hear back right away. Can we talk about ways to reassure each other in these situations?"

Nagging Thought: *Did I say something wrong? I keep replaying the conversation.*

Reframe: "Over-analyzing won't change the past. If I'm unsure, I can ask instead of assuming."

How to Discuss: "Sometimes I overthink what I say and worry I may have upset you. If something bothers you, I'd love for us to be open about it."

Nagging Thought: *They're acting differently today. Maybe they don't love me anymore.*

Reframe: "People have mood swings. It's not always about me."

How to Discuss: "I noticed you seem a bit off today. Is everything okay, or is there something on your mind you'd like to share?"

Nagging Thought: *I need to explain myself fully so they don't misunderstand me.*

Reframe: "It's okay to communicate simply and trust that they'll ask for clarity if needed."

How to Discuss: "I sometimes feel the need to over-explain to avoid misunderstandings. Can we talk about how we can both feel heard and understood without overcomplicating things?"

Nagging Thought: *They complimented me, but did they really mean it?*

Reframe: "I'll choose to accept compliments without second-guessing their sincerity."

How to Discuss: "I struggle with accepting compliments and doubt them. Can you help me by reassuring me that your words are genuine?"

Nagging Thought: *If I don't hear 'I love you' often, do they still care?*

Reframe: People show love in different ways, not just in words.

How to Discuss: "I love hearing 'I love you' and it reassures me. How do you like to express love, and is it okay if I ask for verbal affirmations sometimes?"

Nagging Thought: *If I bring up my feelings, I'll seem needy or push them away.*

Reframe: "Expressing feelings is healthy. A good relationship allows space for honesty."

How to Discuss: "I sometimes worry that sharing my feelings might overwhelm you. How can we make sure we both feel comfortable discussing emotions?"

Nagging Thought: *They liked someone's photo on social media—what does that mean?*

Reframe: "A like is just a like. I won't create stories in my head without actual evidence."

How to Discuss: "I've noticed I feel uneasy about social media interactions. Can we talk about our boundaries and how we can reassure each other?"

Nagging Thought: *What if they leave me one day?*

Reframe: "Worrying about the future doesn't prevent pain. I'll focus on building a healthy relationship now."

How to Discuss: "I sometimes fear losing you, and I know that's my anxiety talking. Can we discuss ways to reassure each other about our commitment?"

Nagging Thought: *I should be able to read their mind so I don't upset them.*

Reframe: "Nobody is a mind reader. It's better to communicate openly than assume."

How to Discuss: "I want to be attentive to your feelings, but I realize I can't always guess them. Can we commit to expressing our needs clearly to each other?"

QUIZ: Is Overthinking Hurting Your Relationship?

Answer these questions with what comes to your mind first:

1. When your partner doesn't reply to a message quickly, do you:

    - A) Assume they're busy and wait.

    - B) Feel a little anxious but try to distract yourself.

    - C) Worry something is wrong and check their activity online.

2. Do you frequently replay past conversations in your mind, wondering if you said something wrong?

    - A) Rarely

- B) Sometimes
- C) All the time

3. If your partner seems quieter than usual, do you:
    - A) Assume they have personal stuff on their mind.
    - B) Feel uneasy but wait to see if they open up.
    - C) Start worrying they might be upset with you.

4. Do you find yourself over-explaining your feelings to avoid misunderstandings?
    - A) No, I communicate simply.
    - B) Sometimes, depending on the situation.
    - C) Yes, I always try to clarify everything.

5. When your partner compliments you, do you:
    - A) Accept it and feel good.
    - B) Appreciate it but still wonder if they mean it.
    - C) Overthink it and feel suspicious.

6. If your partner is out with friends, do you:
    - A) Enjoy your own time and trust them.
    - B) Feel a little uneasy but remind yourself everything is fine.
    - C) Check their social media for reassurance.

7. Do you fear that bringing up concerns might push your partner

away?

- A) No, I believe open communication is important.
- B) Sometimes, but I try to speak up.
- C) Yes, I avoid tough conversations.

Results:

- **Mostly A's:** You have a healthy approach to relationship thoughts! Keep trusting yourself.

- **Mostly B's:** You overthink at times, but you're self-aware and working on it.

- **Mostly C's:** Overthinking may be creating stress in your relationship. It might be time to work on letting go of unnecessary worries.

Want practical strategies to overcome overthinking? **Get your copy of** *The Overthinker's Guide to Relationship Communication* today!

https://www.amazon.com/dp/B0DNTGP7W8

Conclusion

"Our brain is an extraordinarily helpful tool, but when we overthink, we only undermine its power." - Nick Trenton

We often don't clearly speak our truth to each other. We speak in nuance and metaphors, drop hints, and offer clues to decipher with our body language. We think that we are being gentle. We believe that if they are smart or tuned in if they care, they'll definitely see the signs.

Over time, these codes become our comfort zone, a safe distance from which to test the waters of vulnerability. It's easier to hint at our needs than to state them plainly. It is easier to hope someone reads between our lines than to write them.

The most brutal truth to learn about relationships is that clarity can feel harsh when we're used to softening our words. Being direct can feel like being mean when we've mastered the art of gentle hints. But perhaps the real callousness lies in expecting our partners to be mind readers, in making them guess at the contents of our hearts.

We now know that love doesn't mean someone anticipates our needs before they are communicated. Real intimacy grows in the space between speaking our truth and hearing others'. It grows when we choose clarity over comfort and straightforwardness over safety.

This isn't about becoming different people. It's about becoming more straightforward versions of ourselves, saying what we mean, asking for what we need, and creating relationships built on understanding rather than assumption.

The rest is up to you.

References

1. Acosta, K.(2022, January 11). *What causes overthinking—and 6 ways to stop*. Forbes Health. https://www.forbes.com/health/mind/what-causes-overthinking-and-6-ways-to-stop/

2. Cassidy, J.,& Shaver, P. R. (Eds.). (2016). *Handbook of attachment: Theory, research, and clinical applications* (3rd ed.). Guilford Press.

3. *Codependency*. (n.d.). Psychology Today.https://www.psychologytoday.com/za/basics/codependency

4. Doulike.(2019). *Interracial marriage statistics*. Retrieved from https://www.doulike.com/blog/marriage/interracial-marriage-statistics/

5. *Empathy: Better with boundaries*. (2023,October 24). Heidi Goehmann.https://heidigoehmann.com/articles/empathy-better-with-boundaries

6. Fidelman, M.(2023, May 10). *100quotes about overthinking to help you calm your mind*. Parade.Retrieved from https://parade.com/living/overthinking-quotes#quotes-about-the-impact-of-overthinking

7. Field, B.(n.d.). *How to set relationship goals with your partner*. Very well Mind.https://www.verywellmind.com/how-to-set-relation

ship-goals-with-your-partner-7547010

8. Glassie SL, Schutte NS. The relationship between emotional intelligence and optimism: A meta-analysis. Int J Psychol. 2024Jun;59(3):353-367. doi: 10.1002/ijop.13108. Epub 2024 Jan 12. PMID: 38216335.

9. Gould, W. R.(2020, December 8). *What is codependency?*Verywell Mind. https://www.verywellmind.com/what-is-codependency-5072124

10. Hexpoor, M.(n.d.). *Six ways for empaths to set healthy boundaries.* LinkedIn.https://www.linkedin.com/pulse/6-ways-empaths-set-healthy-boundaries-minou-hexspoor-pcc-eli-mp/

11. *How to stop overthinking in a relationship five tips and signs.* (2023, July17). Anchor Light Therapy Collective.https://anchorlighttherapy.com/overthinking-in-a-relationship/

12. Ivtzan, I.(2024). *How to set boundaries for your empathy.* Psychology Today.https://www.psychologytoday.com/za/blog/mindfulness-for-wellbeing/202406/how-to-set-boundaries-for-your-empathy

13. Jiang H, Wang W, Mei Y, Zhao Z, Lin B, Zhang Z. A scoping review of the self-reported compassion measurement tools. BMC Public Health.2023 Nov 24;23(1):2323. doi: 10.1186/s12889-023-17178-2. PMID: 37996796; PMCID:PMC10668436.

14. Lawrence, L.(2022, October 20). *What is a codependent relationship? Could I be in one?* Healthline.https://www.healthline.com/health/relationships/codependent-relationship

15. Leonard, E.(2021). *How to firm up your boundaries while keeping*

a kind heart. Psychology Today.https://www.psychologytoday.com/intl/blog/peaceful-parenting/202107/how-to-firm-up-your-boundaries-while-keeping-a-kind-heart

16. Liles, M.(2023, March 22). *Fifty relationship goals that'll help you grow closer as a couple.* Parade.https://parade.com/1339937/marynliles/relationship-goals/

17. Lupcho, T.(2023, February 23). *How to stop overthinking in a relationship.* Https://Thriveworks.com/.https://thriveworks.com/help-with-relationships/how-to-stop-overthinking-in-a-relationship/

18. Medcalf, A.(2019, January 1). *The truth about setting relationship goals.* Abby Medcalf.https://abbymedcalf.com/the-truth-about-setting-relationship-goals/

19. Merriam-Webster.(n.d.). *[Word].*In *Merriam-Webster.com dictionary.* Retrieved [Date], from https://www.merriam-webster.com/dictionary/overthinking

20. Munoz, A.(2022, November 8). How to stop overthinking your relationship. *Cal Alumni Association.*https://greatergood.berkeley.edu/article/item/how_to_stop_overthinking_your_relationship

21. Neff K. Self-Compassion: an alternative conceptualization of a healthy attitude toward oneself. Self and Identity.2003;2(2):85–101. doi: 10.1080/15298860309032.

22. Neff, K. D.(2003). Development and validation of a scale to measure self-compassion. Selfand Identity, 2, 223-250.

23. *No worries wellness LLC.* (2021, September 15). No Worries

Wellness LLC.https://noworrieswellness.org/noworries-blog/why-we-overthink-and-8-ways-to-stop-overthinking#google_vignette

24. Pew Research Center. (2017, May 18). *Intermarriage in the U.S. 50 years after Loving v. Virginia*.Retrieved from https://www.pewresearch.org/social-trends/2017/05/18/intermarriage-in-the-u-s-50-years-after-loving-v-virginia/

25. Reid, S.(2022, March 4). *Codependency: Signs of a codependent relationship.* HelpGuide.https://www.helpguide.org/relationships/social-connection/codependency

26. Scourfield,D. (2021, June 16). *Why empathy without boundaries is a self-destructive act.* Camino Recovery Spain.https://www.caminorecovery.com/blog/why-empathy-without-boundaries-is-a-self-destructive-act/

27. SharonSalzberg. (n.d.). *Three steps for self-compassion, illustrated. Lion's Roar.* Retrieved November 18, 2024, from https://www.lionsroar.com/three-steps-for-self-compassion-illustrated/

28. Sullivan, M.(2023, June 13). *Here's how to stop overthinking your relationship.* Cosmopolitan.https://www.cosmopolitan.com/sex-love/a44178497/how-to-stop-overthinking-your-relationship/

29. Tai, T.(2022, November 28). *Goal setting for couples: 10 tips to set better goals with your partner.* His & Her Money. https://www.hisandhermoney.com/goal-setting-for-couples/

30. Mind Remake Project. (2021, June 14). *My Life Meditation app (formerly Stop, Breathe & Think).* Retrieved from https://mindremakeproject.org/2021/06/14/top-free-apps-for-meditation/

31. Mindful. (n.d.). *Mindfulness.com: Mindfulness and meditation*

for all levels. Retrieved from https://www.mindful.org/free-mindfulness-apps-worthy-of-your-attention/

32. Mindful. (n.d.). *Smiling Mind: Free mindfulness app for all ages*. Retrieved from https://www.mindful.org/free-mindfulness-apps-worthy-of-your-attention/

33. Reader's Digest. (n.d.). *Insight Timer: Free meditation app*. Retrieved from https://www.rd.com/list/free-meditation-apps/

34. UCLA Health. (n.d.). *UCLA Mindful:Free guided meditations by the UCLA Mindful Awareness Research Center*.Retrieved from https://www.uclahealth.org/programs/uclamindful/free-guided-meditations/guided-meditations

www.ingramcontent.com/pod-product-compliance
Lightning Source LLC
Chambersburg PA
CBHW020544030426
42337CB00013B/965